HURRICANES

DANGEROUS WEATHER

HURRICANES

Michael Allaby

Facts On File, Inc.

HURRICANES

Copyright © 1997 by Michael Allaby

Facts On File, Inc.
11 Penn Plaza
New York NY 10001

Library of Congress Cataloging-in-Publication Data
Allaby, Michael.
   Hurricanes / Michael Allaby.
      p.   cm. — (Dangerous weather)
   Includes index.
   ISBN 0-8160-3516-4 (acid-free paper)
   1. Hurricanes. I. Title. II. Series: Allaby, Michael.
Dangerous weather.
QC944.A44   1997
551.55'232—dc20   96-22475

Text design by Richard Garratt
Cover design by Matt Galemmo
Illustrations by Richard Garratt

Printed in the United States of America

RRD FOF 10 9 8 7 6 5 4 3

Contents

HURRICANES

What is a hurricane?

It begins far out at sea, over the Caribbean. At first it amounts to not very much, merely a body of air in which the atmospheric pressure is lower than in the surrounding air. This is a depression. Had it formed further north, say at around 50°, it would be no different from the many depressions that each year drift eastward across the Atlantic. Some fill, as air flows into them, increasing the pressure until it is the same as that of the surrounding air, and no more is heard of them. Others bring gray weather, with rain or snow, to northwestern Europe. If there is a large difference in pressure between the depression and the surrounding air, they may also bring wind to drive the rain and make sure anyone caught outdoors without waterproof clothing is thoroughly soaked. They are unpleasant, but that is all. They cause no harm. They are not dangerous.

But this is not 50° N. It is the Caribbean, in the tropics, and already the depression is being watched carefully. High above, a satellite transmits photographs of the clouds forming inside it to meteorologists on the ground. These allow the scientists to trace its development and track its movements. Ships and aircraft passing through the depression radio measurements of its winds, pressure, and air temperature to the weather center. Perhaps it will fill. In that case it and

Figure 1: *The Holiday Inn at Cutter Ridge, north of Homestead, Florida, suffered extensive wind damage during Hurricane Andrew. Nearly every window was blown out.* (National Oceanic and Atmospheric Administration [NOAA])

the clouds it produces will vanish from the pictures.

This depression does not fill. The pressure at its center falls further. After a couple of days it has dropped by 20 millibars. Again, a drop in pressure of this magnitude is not uncommon in middle latitudes, but in the tropics it is unusual. At this point the meteorologists start to pay even closer attention.

As air pressure falls, the depression begins to turn, rotating around its own center, and the prevailing easterly winds start to carry it westward. Air drawn into the region of low pressure flows counterclockwise around the center, its speed proportional to the difference in pressure inside and outside the depression. Falling pressure causes wind speeds to increase.

Clouds grow around the center, forming great, towering masses. Seen from space, they form a spiral shape. Beneath them, rain is falling heavily. When the wind speed exceeds about 25 MPH the weather system is officially classified as a tropical depression and identified by a number; for example, TD14. When it exceeds about 40 MPH it becomes a tropical storm and may be given a name.

Tropical storms are fairly common during the summer and fall. In October 1995, 19 were recorded.

Pressure continues to fall and wind speeds continue to increase. When they exceed 74 MPH the tropical storm becomes a hurricane.

Still it is moving westward and still it is strengthening. Now the spiral of cloud is about 125 miles in diameter. As it approaches the first of the inhabited Caribbean islands it begins to swing north.

Figure 2: *Wind speeds around a hurricane.*

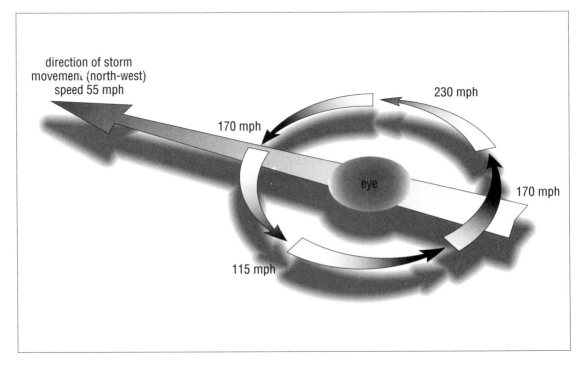

direction of storm movement (north-west) speed 55 mph

230 mph

170 mph

eye

170 mph

115 mph

It arrives with torrential rain and a screaming wind. Trees are uprooted and thrown about like sticks. Flimsy buildings are demolished. Roofs are lifted from more substantial houses, cars and trucks are overturned, windows are shattered, and flying debris adds to the damage caused by the wind itself.

Then the sea arrives. Driven by the wind, huge waves sweep over low-lying coastal areas. Winds of more than 100 MPH can raise 15-foot waves and these may combine with the tide to produce a massive storm surge, with spray and foam blowing still further inland.

By now the hurricane has reached its maximum ferocity. Its winds are much stronger on the right-hand side than on the left-hand side. As the diagram shows, this is because the hurricane itself is moving in a generally westward direction. To the right of its center, the speed of its own movement adds to the wind speed. To its left, the wind blows in the opposite direction to that in which the hurricane is traveling, so wind speed is reduced.

It turns north, heading now towards the coast of the United States and devastating the islands in its path. Hurricane Opal, which struck Guatemala, Mexico, and Florida in early October 1995 with 150-MPH winds, caused 63 deaths and damage estimated to cost $4 billion. In 1900, a hurricane caused 6,000 deaths in Galveston, Texas.

Once it moves inland, however, the hurricane is doomed. It needs water to sustain it and away from the sea it is starved. Slowly it weakens and eventually dies, although it may retain enough force to cause substantial damage as far north as Pennsylvania.

A hurricane releases no radiation, of course, but it may have as much energy as a one-megaton hydrogen bomb and it can be as destructive. It is the largest, fiercest storm our atmosphere is capable of producing.

Ocean currents and sea-surface temperature

Our planet is warmed by the Sun, but it is not warmed evenly. The equator faces the Sun directly, and the tropics, where the Sun is directly overhead at noon on at least one day in the year, receive much more energy than do the polar regions where on at least one day each year the Sun never rises above the horizon and on at least one day each year it does not descend below it (see box). It is not surprising, therefore, that the tropics enjoy a warm climate and the Arctic and Antarctic are cold. If the Earth had no atmosphere and no liquid water at its surface, these differences would be much

Global circulation of the atmosphere

The tropics, of Cancer in the north and Capricorn in the south, mark the boundaries of the belt around the Earth where the Sun is directly overhead at noon on at least one day in the year. The Arctic and Antarctic Circles mark the boundaries of regions in which the Sun does not rise above the horizon on at least one day of the year and does not sink below the horizon on at least one day in the year.

Imagine a beam of sunlight just a few degrees wide. As the drawing shows, this beam illuminates a much smaller area if the Sun is directly overhead than it does if the Sun is at a low angle in the sky. The amount of energy in each beam is the same because they are of the same width, so energy is spread over a smaller area directly beneath the Sun than it is when the Sun is lower. This is why the tropics are heated more strongly than any other part of the Earth and the amount of heat we receive from the Sun decreases the further we are from the equator.

Solar energy warms the surface of land and water. The air is warmed by contact with the surface. As it is warmed, the air expands. This makes it less dense than the air immediately above it, so it rises, its place near the surface being taken by denser air flowing inward. This air is heated in its turn.

Where the surface is heated strongly and air in contact with it is expanding, there will be a region of low surface atmospheric pressure. The equatorial belt is a region of generally low pressure.

At high altitude, the rising air cools, becomes more dense, and sinks. Where the sinking air reaches the surface the atmospheric pressure will be high. The edges of the tropics and the subtropics, where equatorial air is sinking, are regions of generally high pressure, one in each hemisphere. Although the air is very cold while it remains at a great height, as it sinks and is compressed it warms *adiabatically* (without mixing with surrounding air), so air in the tropical-subtropical regions is warm.

Global distribution of pressure.

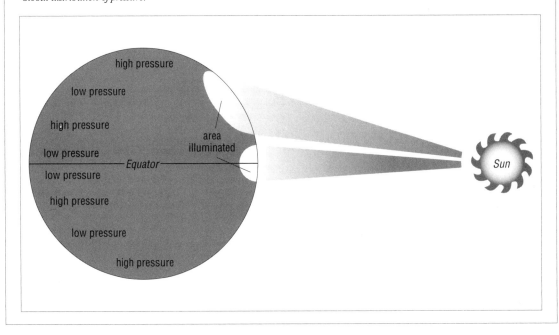

Over the poles, very cold air sinks to the surface. This produces generally high pressure.

Between the low-latitude high pressure and the high-latitude high pressure there is, in each hemisphere, a belt of generally low pressure.

Air movements carry warm air away from the tropics and cool air away from polar regions. This distributes the warmth we receive from the Sun more evenly than would be possible if the Earth had no atmosphere.

Although the Earth is heated most strongly in the tropics, all parts of the planet receive some warmth from the Sun, and land and water respond differently. Land warms and cools much faster than water. As air moves, it is warmed or cooled by the surface over which it travels.

Together, the transport of heat from low to high latitudes and the difference in the effect of heating on land and water generate the global circulation of the atmosphere. It is this circulation that produces regional climates and our day-to-day weather.

greater, and the difference in temperature between day and night would be as extreme as it is on the Moon, where the maximum daytime temperature is about 230° F and the minimum night-time temperature about –275° F. The Moon has no atmosphere to speak of (there is a very thin atmosphere, amounting to a few gas molecules in every cubic inch of space close to the surface). On Earth, however, the Sun warms the surface of land and sea, and the air is heated by contact with the warmed surface. Air and water can move, and in doing so they transport warmth away from the equator, warming the cold places and cooling the hot places.

When it is warm or cold, when the Sun shines or when it is cloudy, and when it rains or snows, naturally we assume it is the air that brings us our weather. This is true, of course, but the oceans play a very important part. Scientists have known for many years that, like moving air, ocean currents transport heat from the tropics to high latitudes, but they now realize that the oceans have an even greater influence on the climates of the world than they had previously supposed.

That influence is due to certain remarkable properties of water. The first of these is its *thermal capacity*. This is the amount of heat energy that must be applied to a given mass of a substance to raise its temperature by a specified amount. Water has a very high thermal capacity. At 59° F, which is the average temperature at the surface of the Earth, it requires 51 calories of heat to raise the temperature of one ounce of water by one degree Fahrenheit (4.1855 joules per gram per degree Celsius). This means that water absorbs a large amount of heat before its temperature changes at all, and then it warms only slowly. Its thermal capacity varies at different temperatures, but only very slightly. Dry soil, with a thermal capacity of about 10 calories per ounce per degree Fahrenheit, warms much more quickly than water. Air, passing from land to sea in summer, is warmed by contact with the land, then cooled as it passes over the sea.

Their different thermal capacities also mean that water is much slower than dry land to give up its heat. In winter, air may be warmed as it passes over the ocean and cooled when it crosses land.

Water moderates climates because of its high thermal capacity. It slows the rate of summer warming by absorbing heat with little change in its own temperature and it slows the rate of winter cooling by gradually releasing the heat it spent the summer absorbing. By late fall, the sea-surface temperature in the northern North Atlantic is usually a few degrees higher than the air temperature over adjacent land.

Oceans cover about 70% of the Earth to an average depth of more than 12,000 feet. Their total volume is more than 325 million cubic miles. That is a very large amount of water spread over a very large area. Consequently, its moderating effect on climate is huge.

This is only one way the oceans influence the global climate. They also move heat from low to high latitudes by themselves, independently of the air.

Water near the equator is strongly warmed by the Sun and flows north and south away from the equator as warm currents, its place being taken by cold currents flowing away from the poles. Air passing over a warm current is warmed by it. The average winter temperature in Britain, for example, is 27° F higher than that in Newfoundland, in about the same latitude, because the British coast is bathed by the extension of the warm Gulf Stream known as the North Atlantic Drift and Newfoundland is washed by the cold Labrador Current flowing south from the Arctic.

The Gulf Stream and North Atlantic Drift form part of a *gyre,* a large-scale system of currents flowing in a clockwise direction around the North Atlantic. The map shows the principal components of this system. It begins just north of the equator as the westward-flowing North Equatorial Current. This turns north off the North American coast, becoming the Antilles Current (not named on the map) and then the Florida Current, and as it passes the Gulf of Mexico it becomes known as the Gulf Stream, with the still waters of the Sargasso Sea bordering it to the east. At about 40° N, in the latitude of Spain and Portugal, it turns east across the ocean and then south, returning to the tropics to become the North Equatorial Current again and joining the Equatorial Counter Current. At about 40° N the Gulf Stream divides and the North Atlantic Drift heads away in a northeasterly direction, washing the coast of Northwest Europe and passing around the north coast of Norway, where it becomes the Norwegian Current flowing into the Arctic. The Arctic is warmer than the Antarctic because it is covered mainly by sea fed

(Opposite) Figure 3:
Principal Atlantic currents.

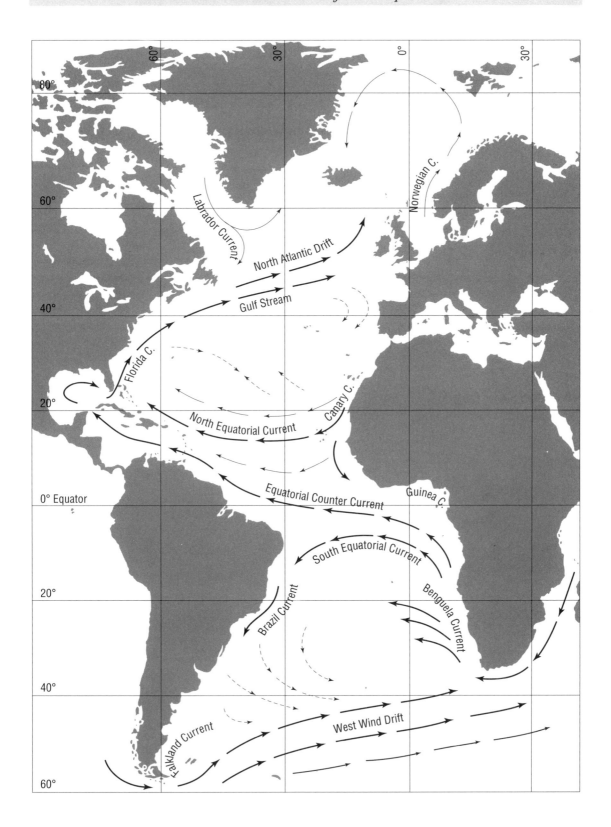

by warm currents. The Antarctic is dominated by the huge continent of Antarctica.

This gyre strongly affects the climates of lands bordering the North Atlantic and it forms part of the *Atlantic conveyor,* an even bigger system that influences climates over much of the world. The conveyor begins near the Arctic Circle, where ice forms on the sea surface. What happens next is due to two of the more remarkable properties of water.

As the temperature of water falls, its molecules lose energy and move more slowly. This causes them to crowd together more closely, so that a given volume of water contains more of them. The water then weighs more as its density increases, reaching a maximum at about 40° F. Below this temperature, ice starts to form as water molecules arrange themselves into crystals that are open at the center. Because ice crystals are open, freezing makes water expand and its density decreases. Ice is less dense than water just above freezing temperature, which is why ice floats. At the edge of the sea ice and just beneath it, water just a little above freezing temperature is denser than the warmer water around it.

At the same time, as ice crystals form in salt water, the water molecules bond to one another directly. This breaks the bonds they had with the sodium and chlorine of salt. The ice is made from fresh water and the salt removed from it makes the adjacent water saltier. Salt water is denser than fresh water, because a given volume contains as many water molecules as a similar volume of fresh water at the same temperature, but also the sodium and chlorine atoms of the salt dissolved in it.

Colder and saltier than the surrounding water, the water at the edge of the sea ice sinks all the way to the ocean floor, forming a current flowing south that is known as the North Atlantic Deep Water (NADW). The NADW flows all the way to Antarctica, where it turns and starts to flow north again, back toward the equator, as the Benguela Current passing the west coast of Africa. In the northern ocean, the sinking water is replaced by surface water flowing north. That water comes from lower, warmer latitudes. This is the Atlantic conveyor mechanism that drives the North Atlantic gyre.

It is a slow process. Deep-water currents flow very slowly, perhaps no more than about 150 feet a day, and once it has descended to the ocean floor, the water does not mix with surface water. In the Atlantic, it takes 500 to 800 years for deep water to return to the surface (and in the Pacific it takes twice as long). The Gulf Stream, in contrast, flows at about 6 MPH as a set of narrow streams.

Throughout the whole of human history, the conveyor has remained stable. It has always flowed just as it flows now, but this was not so in the more remote past. Then it changed at intervals, and quickly. Sometimes it flowed more strongly, sometimes it

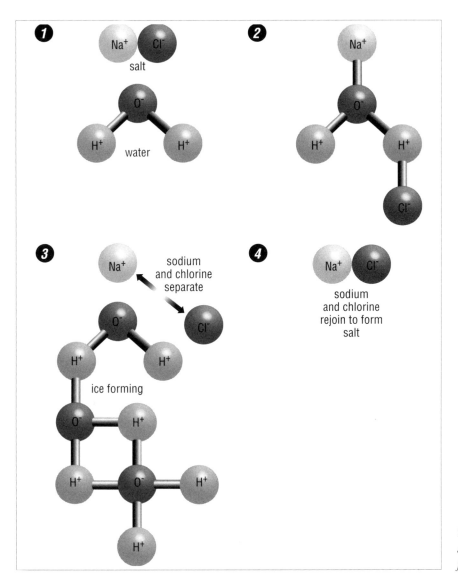

Figure 4: *How dissolved salt separates when water freezes.*

ceased to flow altogether, and its variations wrought major climatic changes. About 10,000 years ago, which is the last time it departed from the behavior we now think of as normal, the North Atlantic Drift ceased to flow and within a few decades the whole of the northern hemisphere was plunged into near ice-age conditions. That change, and probably others that preceded it, was caused by fresh meltwater flowing into the North Atlantic, in that case from the retreat of the ice sheet over North America at the end of the most recent ice age, at other times by the sudden release of large numbers of huge icebergs for reasons scientists are at present unable to explain. Being less dense, the fresh water floated above the salt water like a huge raft. When it froze, no salt was added to the adjacent water. It became denser as it cooled, but not so dense as the salt water beneath it. This prevented dense water continually sinking to form the NADW. Scientists now think that a decrease of less than 1% in the salinity of the North Atlantic might disrupt the conveyor again. This could happen if global warming increased the amount of rain and snow falling at high latitudes.

The gyre drives the circulation, but other surface currents are driven by the wind. To either side of the equator, the winds blow predominantly from the east. These are the *trade winds*, from the northeast in the northern hemisphere and from the southeast in the southern hemisphere. It is the trade winds that drive the equatorial currents in both hemispheres.

There are also gyres, driven by the trade winds, in the South Atlantic and the North and South Pacific, and a smaller and rather more complex one in the southern part of the Indian Ocean. In the North Pacific, the Kuroshio Current is very similar to the Gulf Stream and flows at a similar speed, washing the shores of Japan. In the northern hemisphere all the gyres flow in a clockwise direction, and in the southern hemisphere they flow counterclockwise.

There are regions in the tropics, however, where winds are usually light and often do not blow at all. They are places where the Sun beats down mercilessly, often in very still air. In the days of sailing ships, sailors dreaded these areas and tried to avoid them, because ships could be becalmed there for weeks on end. Sailors called these places the *doldrums* (see box). Both they and the trade winds are produced by the convective circulation of tropical and subtropical air in *Hadley cells* (see box on page 20).

Thousands of feet below the surface of the sea, cold, dense water flows south and its replacement causes the general circulation of ocean water. At the surface, water is also driven by the trade winds. The resulting currents carry away water that has been heated by the tropical Sun, so although tropical waters are always warm, they are cooler than they would be were they not constantly moving and being replaced by cooler water flowing in from higher latitudes.

In the doldrums, however, the lack of wind means the surface water is not moving so fast. It remains exposed to the hot Sun longer, and from time to time patches of it become very warm indeed. If the sea-surface temperature rises above about 80° F over a large area, the scene may be set for a hurricane to develop in the air warmed by contact with the sea. The warm area must lie far enough from the equator (at least 5°, north or south) for the Coriolis effect to be significant (the effect is zero at the equator) (see box on page 40), and it is unlikely to be found further away than about 20°. A warm sea area in the right place is not the only condition necessary for a hurricane to form, but it is probably the most important one.

Trade winds and doldrums

At the tropical margins of the Hadley cells (regions on either side of the equator between 0°–30° latitude), air is sinking. It warms adiabatically as it sinks, but gathers no moisture, so by the time it reaches the surface it is hot and dry. When it reaches the surface, the air diverges, some flowing toward the equator, some away from it. The air flowing toward the equator is swung to the right in the northern hemisphere and to the left in the southern, producing northeasterly winds to the north of the equator and southeasterly winds to its south. These are the *trade winds*.

The name arises from their great importance to sailors in the days when sailing ships plied the oceans. The trade winds occur over nearly half the world and they are very reliable, in speed as well as direction, although they are stronger in winter than in summer.

There is not one Hadley cell, however, but several. This means that the trade winds blow from the eastern margin of each cell (in both hemispheres). They converge where they meet, near the equator, but if you picture the winds as arrows, there are gaps between their "shafts." In these gaps the winds are very light and variable. Often the air is quite still. Ships could be becalmed in these regions. This was not merely inconvenient; so far as the sailors were concerned, it was dangerous. They could sit, day after day, under the scorching heat of the Sun, while their supply of fresh water dwindled. They called these areas the *doldrums* or *horse latitudes* because they would sometimes throw horses overboard to lighten the ship in the hope of reducing the amount of wind needed to carry them to a region of stronger winds.

Trade winds and doldrums.

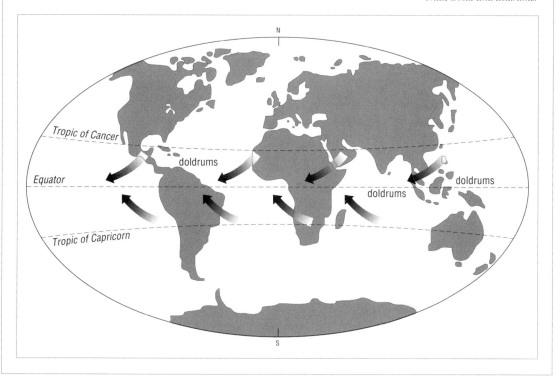

There are no seasons at the equator, but there are in the tropics to its north and south and it is during the tropical summer that the sea is heated most strongly. Because of the high thermal capacity of water, the sea warms slowly through the summer and temperatures high enough to trigger the development of hurricanes are reached at mid to late summer, so hurricanes are most likely in the late summer and fall. In the western Atlantic and Caribbean, and also in the western Pacific, July to October is the peak season for hurricanes, although they can occur as early as May and as late as December; they are most frequent from September to November in Southeast Asia and between April and June and again in October and November in the Indian Ocean. December to March is the hurricane season throughout the southern hemisphere, but hurricanes never develop in the Atlantic south of the equator. In the world as a whole, there are about 80 hurricanes in most years, although 1995 was an exceptional year, with more hurricanes than there had been for more than 60 years and, for the first time in more than 70 years, four named tropical storms in the Atlantic at the same time.

Outside the tropics, hurricanes cannot develop because the sea is never warm enough. They are exclusively tropical, but once formed, hurricanes can travel long distances and sometimes do. Living outside the tropics does not guarantee protection from these fiercest of all tropical storms. Occasionally they reach northern Europe, much weakened after so long a journey, but still with enough energy to wreak considerable havoc, and made worse because Europeans do not expect them, prepare inadequately if at all, and are taken by surprise.

Warming, convection, and low pressure

Before airplanes were invented, there were many arguments among scientists and engineers about the feasibility of building a flying machine that is heavier than air. Some scientists said the whole idea was ridiculous. Then the Wright brothers proved them wrong.

"Lighter-than-air" machines were the alternative to "heavier-than-air" machines and the two varieties competed vigorously for many years. Airships entered passenger service, and in 1936 the German *Hindenburg* began carrying passengers between Germany and the United States. It was not until several airships crashed in the 1930s, culminating in the disaster of the *Hindenburg* at Lakehurst, New Jersey, on May 6, 1937, that people began to think "heavier-than-air" airplanes were safer.

Airships were big. The *Hindenburg* was 804 feet long, powered by four 1,100-horsepower diesel engines, and carried up to 50 passengers in considerable comfort. It carried fuel for its engines, and because the North Atlantic crossing took about 65 hours, food and sleeping accommodation for its crew and passengers. Clearly it was heavier than air, but its engines and cabins were housed in a structure below the main hull and it was the hull that accounted for almost all of its great size. The hull was filled with hydrogen. Modern airships (for the craft are making something of a comeback) use helium. This is more expensive than hydrogen but has the great advantage of being nonflammable. Both hydrogen and helium are lighter than the nitrogen and oxygen of which air is composed, and the difference in weight between the gas in the hull and an equivalent volume of air is equal to the weight of the hull, engines, and accommodation. An airship is made from materials weighing more than air, but the "lifting gas" compensates for their weight.

In effect, an airship is a balloon equipped with engines and that can be steered. Some balloons also use helium as a lifting gas, but most do not. Ballooning has become a popular sport, and the balloons that drift peacefully across the countryside in summer are kept aloft by air itself. They are *hot-air* balloons.

Below the envelope of the balloon itself is the basket in which the passengers ride and immediately above the basket is a powerful burner, fueled by gas. When the burner fires, hot air rises into the envelope and the balloon rises. When the burner is not lit, the air in the envelope slowly cools and the balloon starts to descend.

Like an airship, a balloon has weight, but unlike an airship, a hot-air balloon uses no lifting gas that is lighter than air. It is lifted by air itself. This is possible because when air is heated its density decreases. The principle underlying this was discovered in 1787 by the French physicist Jacques A. C. Charles (1746–1823) and confirmed more accurately in 1802 by another French physicist, Joseph L. Gay-Lussac (1778–1850), so some people call it *Charles's law* and others *Gay-Lussac's law*. It states that if a given mass of gas is held at constant pressure, its volume is proportional to its temperature. This is expressed mathematically as $V = kT$, where V is the volume, T is the temperature measured in kelvins (1K = 1° C = 1.8° F), and k is a constant. If the gas is heated, therefore, it will expand to occupy a larger volume of space. It follows that the original volume will contain less of the heated gas and, because it contains less gas, it will have less mass and so it will weigh less.

Air is a mixture of gases. These exist as molecules moving freely in all directions. They collide with one another frequently and ricochet in new directions. The speed at which they travel depends on their temperature. Heat is a form of energy and when gas molecules absorb it, that energy changes from heat into energy of motion (called *kinetic* energy). When molecules are traveling faster,

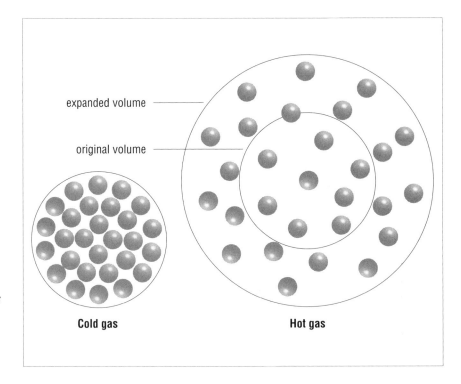

Figure 5: *Effects of heating a gas. In the hot gas, the same number of molecules occupy a bigger volume. The original volume contains fewer molecules, so it weighs less.*

collisions between them are more violent and they ricochet further. This causes them to move, or be "bounced," further apart. The distance between them increases. That is why gas expands when it is heated and why a given volume of hot gas contains fewer molecules than a similar volume of cold gas.

Figure 5 illustrates what happens and it is very easy to demonstrate for yourself (see the experiment in volume 6). Imagine the molecules in the diagram are contained within the envelope of the hot-air balloon. When the burner fires, hot air expands upward into the envelope. Any volume of it contains fewer molecules than the cooler air around it, so it rises to the top of the envelope and denser, cool air is forced out at the bottom to make room for it. After a short time, the air inside the envelope is less dense than the air outside the envelope, so it weighs less than a similar volume of outside air. Being lighter, the warm air rises like an air bubble rising through a bottle of water. It is trapped inside the envelope, however, so it lifts the entire balloon, envelope, burner, basket, passengers and all. As with the airship, the entire structure is lighter than air because the difference between the weight of the air inside and outside the envelope is equal to that of the other components.

Now think about what happens when the Sun warms the Earth. Radiation from the Sun has very little effect on the gases of the atmosphere. It passes through them as though they were not there and is not absorbed until it reaches the surface of land or water.

There it is absorbed and the surface is warmed. The warmed surface then warms the air in contact with it. Solar radiation always warms air from below, not from above, and it is this that produces our weather.

There is now a layer of air warmed by the surface with which it is in contact. Because the air is warmed it expands, and because it expands, it becomes less dense and weighs less, volume for volume, than the surrounding air. This makes it rise. Its place near the surface is taken by cooler air and this is warmed and rises in its turn. The process continues for as long as the Sun continues to warm the surface, producing a stream of rising air fed from below by inflowing cool air and distributing heat vertically through the atmosphere by convection.

Once air expands and starts to rise it begins cooling again. The temperature in the atmosphere decreases with increasing height above the surface. The rate at which temperature falls is known as the *lapse rate* and averages 3.5° F for every 1,000 feet in dry air and about 3° F per 1,000 feet in moist air. Expanding, rising air, however, cools quite independently of the temperature of the air around it. This is called *adiabatic* cooling and is explained in the box.

Eventually, the temperature of the rising air is similar to that of the surrounding air, so its density and volume-for-volume weight are also similar. When it reaches this height it will rise no further, because it is now denser and heavier than the air immediately above it.

If the air is heated very strongly by its contact with the surface and if the rising air is constantly replenished by more air being warmed beneath it, it may rise to a very great height. In such a case, adiabatic cooling can reduce its temperature to around –74° F at an altitude of about 7 miles. Solar heating is strongest in the tropics, and there warmed air rises to about 11 miles, where the temperature is around –112° F.

Above this height, varying from about 11 miles over the equator and seven miles over the poles, the air temperature no longer falls with increasing height, and at a higher level still it starts increasing as height increases. The region of the atmosphere in which this occurs is called the *stratosphere*, where the air forms layers (*strata*) with little vertical movement. The lower boundary of the strato-sphere, called the *tropopause*, traps rising air so it can rise no further.

In equatorial regions, then, air is being heated strongly at the surface and is rising all the way to the tropopause. In fact, it is not quite so simple. Surface heating accounts only partly for the rising air. It is also heated during its rise, by latent heat released as water vapor condenses (see box on page 16) and, although adiabatic cooling is the most important cause of its fall in temperature with height, there is some mixing of warm, rising air and the cooler, surrounding air, which cools the rising air.

Adiabatic warming and cooling

Air is compressed by the weight of air above it. Imagine a balloon partly inflated with air and made from some substance that totally insulates the air inside. No matter what the temperature outside the balloon, the temperature of the air inside remains the same.

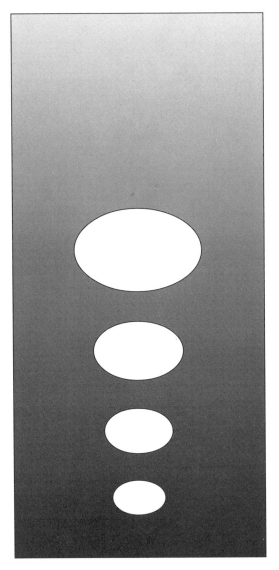

Imagine the balloon is released into the atmosphere. The air inside is squeezed between the weight of air above it, all the way to the top of the atmosphere, and the denser air below it.

Suppose the air inside the balloon is less dense than the air above it. The balloon will rise. As it rises, the distance to the top of the atmosphere becomes smaller, so there is less air above to weigh down on the air in the balloon. At the same time, as it moves through air that is less dense, it experiences less pressure below. This causes the air in the balloon to expand.

When air (or any gas) expands, its molecules move further apart. The *amount* of air remains the same, but it occupies a bigger volume. As they move apart, the molecules must "push" other molecules out of their way. This uses energy, so as the air expands its molecules lose energy. Because they have less energy they move more slowly.

When a moving molecule strikes something, some of its energy of motion (kinetic energy) is transferred to whatever it strikes and part of that energy is converted into heat. This raises the temperature of the struck object by an amount related to the number of molecules striking it and their speed.

In expanding air, the molecules are moving further apart, so a smaller number of them strike an object each second. They are also traveling more slowly, so they strike with less force. This means the temperature of the air decreases. As it expands, air cools.

Effect of air pressure on rising and sinking air. Air is compressed by the weight of air above it. A "parcel" or "bubble" of air is squeezed between the weight of air above and the denser air below. As it rises into a region of less dense air it expands. As it sinks into denser air it contracts.

If the air in the balloon is denser than the air below, it will descend. The pressure on it will increase, its volume will decrease, and its molecules will acquire more energy. Its temperature will increase.

This warming and cooling has nothing to do with the temperature of the air surrounding the balloon. It is called *adiabatic* warming and cooling, from the Greek word *adiabatos*, meaning impassable.

You can easily demonstrate adiabatic cooling and warming for yourself with the experiment described in volume 6.

Wherever you stand on the surface of the Earth, there is a mass of air in what you can imagine as a column extending above you all the way to the top of the atmosphere. Air has weight. This was discovered in 1644, by the Italian physicist Evangelista Torricelli, who worked as an assistant to Galileo and later succeeded him as mathematician to the court of Tuscany. Torricelli invented an instrument to help him decide whether air has weight. The instrument became known as a *barometer* and it is still used today (see volume 6 for more details about Torricelli and barometers).

The weight of air exerts a pressure, just as the weight of any physical object will exert pressure on whatever lies beneath it. Just how much pressure the weight of the air exerts depends on the amount of air present in the column. This can vary. If you climb to the top of a mountain, for example, the column of air above you will be a little shorter, so it will contain less air and the pressure it exerts will be smaller.

Pressure can also vary at sea level, and for the same reason: if the amount of air (the number of air molecules) above a particular place decreases, the air will weigh less and so the surface pressure will decrease. If the amount of air increases, the surface pressure will also increase. Where the surface pressure is lower in one place than in another place nearby, air will flow from the area of high pressure to the area of low pressure, rather like water flowing downhill. This flow of air, from high to low pressure, is what we feel as wind and the strength of the wind varies according to the difference in pressure between the two areas (see box on page 18). A hurricane produces very fierce winds because there is a great difference in pressure between the area covered by the hurricane system and the air surrounding it.

Over equatorial regions, where the surface is being heated strongly throughout the year and air warmed by contact with it is expanding and rising, the air all the way up to the tropopause is less dense than air to the north and south. This means there is less air (fewer air molecules) over equatorial regions than there are elsewhere, and so the surface air pressure is permanently low compared with the pressure elsewhere.

Air pressure, highs, and lows

When air is warmed it expands and becomes less dense. When air is chilled it contracts and becomes more dense.

Air expands by pushing away the air around it. It rises because it is less dense than the air immediately above it. Denser air flows in to replace it, is warmed by contact with the surface, and also expands and rises. Imagine a column of air extending all the way from the surface to the top of the atmosphere. Warming from below causes expansion; as a result, surrounding air is pushed out of the column, so the remaining air is less dense (contains fewer molecules of air) than it did when it was cooler. Because there is less air in the column, the pressure its weight exerts at the surface is reduced. The result is an area of low surface pressure, often called simply a *low*.

In chilled air the opposite happens. The air molecules move closer together, so the air contracts, becomes more dense, and sinks. The amount of air in the column increases, its weight increases, and the surface atmospheric pressure also increases. This produces an area of high pressure, or simply a *high*.

At sea level, the atmosphere exerts sufficient pressure to raise a column of mercury about 30 inches (760 mm) in a tube from which the air has been removed. Meteorologists call this pressure one *bar* and measure atmospheric pressure in *millibars* (1,000 millibars (mb) = 1 bar = 10^6 dynes cm^{-2} = 100,000 pascals).

Air pressure decreases with height because there is less air above to exert pressure. Pressure measured at different places on the surface is corrected to sea-level pressure to remove differences due only to altitude. Lines are then drawn on maps, linking places where the pressure is the same. These lines, called *isobars*, allow meteorologists to study the distribution of pressure.

Like water flowing downhill, air flows from high to low pressure. Its speed, which we feel as wind strength, depends on the difference in pressure between the two regions. This is called the *pressure gradient*. On a weather map it is calculated from the distance between isobars, just as the distance between contours on an ordinary map allows the steepness of hills to be measured. The steeper the gradient the stronger the wind.

Moving air experiences friction with the surface. This slows it more over land, where the friction is greater, than over the sea. Air is also subject to the *Coriolis* effect, which swings it to the right in the northern hemisphere and to the left in the southern hemisphere. As a consequence, winds do not cross the isobars at 90°. Over the oceans they cross at about 30° and over land at about 45°.

Pressure gradient and wind speed (pressures in millibars).

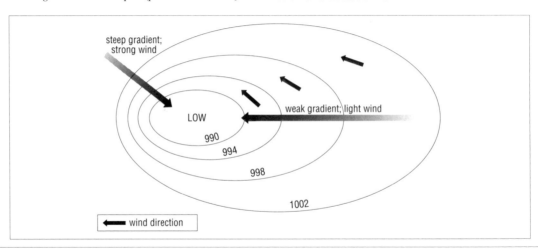

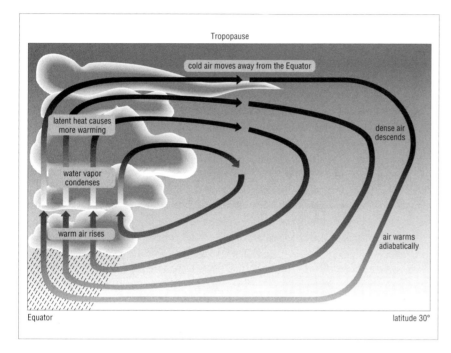

Figure 6: *Cross section of a Hadley cell.*

When it reaches the tropopause and can rise no higher, the equatorial air spreads away from the equator, moving northward in the northern hemisphere and southward in the southern hemisphere. It is now extremely cold because it has cooled adiabatically, and because it is being fed constantly by more rising air, its density increases. The cold air becomes denser, and being denser it becomes heavier, so it sinks.

This air is also very dry. At low levels it is moist because water readily evaporates into it and most of the equatorial regions are covered by ocean. The amount of water vapor that air can carry depends on its temperature, however, and as the rising air cools, more of its water vapor condenses (see box on page 16). By the time it reaches the tropopause it has lost almost all of its water vapor.

Cold, dry, dense air that originated over the equator sinks all the way to the surface in the tropics. As it sinks, it warms adiabatically, so by the time it reaches the surface it is hot, but still very dry. It produces deserts throughout the tropics in both hemispheres. It also produces a region of permanently high surface pressure. Just below the tropopause, air is constantly being fed into the flow from the direction of the equator, increasing the amount (number of molecules) of air between the surface and tropopause and, therefore, its weight and the pressure it exerts at the surface.

At the surface, some of the air moves toward the equator and some moves away from the equator. The air moving away from the equator extends the deserts into higher latitudes. The air moving

George Hadley and Hadley cells

When European ships began venturing far from their home ports, into the tropics and across the equator, sailors learned that the trade winds are very dependable in both strength and direction. They made use of them, and by the end of the 16th century their existence was well known.

Many years passed, however, before anyone knew why the trade winds blow so reliably. Like many scientific explanations, this one developed in stages.

Edmund Halley (1656–1742), the English astronomer, was the first person to offer an explanation. In 1686 he suggested that air at the equator is heated more strongly than air anywhere else. The warm equatorial air rises, cold air flows in near the surface from either side to replace it, and this inflowing air forms

the trade winds. If this were so, however, the trades either side of the equator would flow from due north and south. In fact, they flow from the northeast and southeast.

There the matter rested until 1735. In that year George Hadley (1685–1768), an English meteorologist, proposed a modification of the Halley theory. Hadley agreed that warm equatorial air rises and is replaced at the surface, but said that the rotation of the Earth from west to east swings the moving air, making the winds blow from the northeast and southeast.

Hadley was right about what happened, but not about the reason for it. This was discovered in 1856 by the American meteorologist William Ferrel (1817–91), who said the swing is due to the tendency of moving air to rotate about its own axis, like coffee stirred in a cup.

In accounting for the trade winds, Hadley had proposed a general explanation for the

Three-cell model of atmospheric circulation.

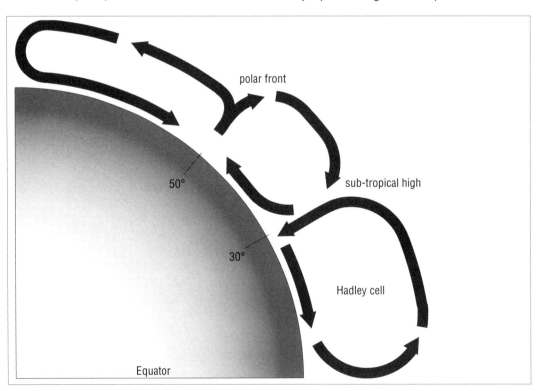

way heat is transported away from the equator. He suggested that the warm equatorial air moves at a great height all the way to the poles, where it descends. When this kind of vertical movement driven by heating from below occurs in a fluid, it is called a *convection cell*; the cell Hadley described is known as a *Hadley cell*.

The rotation of the Earth prevents a single, huge Hadley cell from forming. What really happens is more complicated. In various equatorial regions, warm air rises to a height of about 10 miles, moves away from the equator, cools, and descends between latitudes 25° and 30° N and S. These are the Hadley cells. When it reaches the surface in the tropics, some of the air flows back towards the equator and some flows away from the equator.

Over the poles, cold air descends and flows away from the poles at a low level. At about latitude 50° it meets air flowing away from the equatorial Hadley cells. Where the two types of air meet is called the *polar front*. Air rises again at the polar front. Some flows towards the pole, completing a high-latitude cell, and some flows toward the equator until it meets the descending air of the Hadley cell, which it joins.

There are three sets of cells in each hemisphere. This is called the *three-cell model* of atmospheric circulation by which warm air moves away from the equator and cool air moves toward the equator.

towards the equator replaces the warm, rising air and completes the cycle. Air rises over the equator, moves away from the equator and sinks, then flows back to the equator at a low level.

This pattern of movement is called a *convection cell* and the huge atmospheric convection cell moving air between the equator and tropics is called a *Hadley cell*. Figure 6 shows how it works.

It is called a Hadley cell because it was discovered in the seventeenth century by George Hadley (see the box). Wind is simply air on the move, and Hadley wanted to explain why tropical winds are so reliable. They blow reliably from the northeast in the northern hemisphere and southeast in the southern hemisphere for so much of the time that in the days of sailing ships they came to be known as *trade winds* because they were of such value to trading ships. As the box explains, however, we now know that there is not just one convection cell, as Hadley thought, but three distinct systems of cells together comprising what meteorologists call the *three-cell model* of atmospheric circulation.

The three-cell model explains how heat is carried from equatorial regions into high latitudes. It also explains the general distribution of pressure systems. Wherever air is rising, surface pressure will generally be low, and where air is sinking, surface pressure will be high. Pressure is low in equatorial regions, high in the tropics and subtropics, and high at the poles. In mid-latitudes pressure is very variable. That is where polar air and tropical air meet, at a boundary that moves north and south according to conditions close to the tropopause. This makes mid-latitude weather very changeable and difficult to forecast. Nevertheless, over the region as a whole, pressure is low more often than it is high.

Warm, rising air is what meteorologists call unstable, because it continues to rise until it reaches a level where the surrounding air has the same density as itself. If the air is moist as well as unstable, towering clouds will form in it. These clouds can cause storms anywhere, but near the equator, where the air is moist and more unstable than it is anywhere else on Earth, they can cause hurricanes.

Storm clouds

Rising air cools. As it does so, water vapor in the air may condense into tiny droplets or ice crystals to form clouds. But this is only part of the story. If this were all there is to it, clouds would all be alike and, obviously, they are not. Some are small, white, and puffy, the kind of clouds seen on a fine day in summer and called *fair-weather cumulus*. Clouds may be in flat layers or billowing heaps. There are white clouds, black clouds, and clouds of every imaginable shade of gray. Some clouds bring fine drizzle, some bring rain or snow showers. Other clouds mean torrential rain, snow, or hail, often with thunder and lightning. It is these storm clouds that, in some places and under certain conditions, can cause hurricanes.

Clouds are not all the same and throughout history people tried to find ways to describe the different types clearly. It is not so easy as you might think. In ancient Greece, the philosopher Theophrastus (c. 372–c. 287 B.C.), a student of Plato and friend of Aristotle, wrote of "clouds like fleeces of wool," and "streaks of cloud." Theophrastus was good at classifying things, especially plants. He is often called "the father of botany." Yet classifying clouds defeated him. Jean Lamarck (1744–1829), the French naturalist, was a great naturalist and classifier of plants and animals. He also tried classifying clouds, but with little success. In his system, clouds were described using such words as "sweepings," "bars," "grouped," "piled," "veiled," and "dappled."

It was not until 1803 that Luke Howard, a young apothecary (druggist) living in London, published an article setting out a scheme for classifying clouds that worked and could be made to include every kind of cloud (see volume 6 for more details about Luke Howard and his classification). The classification he devised formed the basis of the one used to this day. All meteorologists use it in a way that is standardized throughout the world by the World Meteorological Organization, which is an agency of the United Nations (see box on page 24), so if you describe a cloud by its proper, scientific name, any meteorologist in the world will know what you mean. The system is used just like the one used to name plants and animals. Every language has its own word for *dog*, but call the animal *Canis familiaris* and zoologists of all nationalities will understand you.

Although the cloud classification is detailed and quite complicated, many of the names it uses describe clouds that are seen only rarely, and then only in some places. There are only ten main cloud types and their names are not hard to remember.

All clouds form by the condensation of water vapor, but the type of cloud that results depends on the height at which it forms and what is happening in the air itself. If the air is being heated strongly from below and is therefore rising, with heat moving vertically by convection, the air is said to be unstable. Heaped clouds of the cumulus type (the adjective is *cumuliform*) will develop in unstable air, and the stronger the vertical movement of air, the taller they will be. If there is little vertical movement, and especially if the air is slowly sinking, it is said to be 'stable.' Layered clouds of the stratus type (the adjective is *stratiform*) will form in stable air. Both cumuliform and stratiform clouds can produce rain or snow, but stratiform clouds usually deliver steady, persistent precipitation and cumuliform clouds produce showers, which can be heavy. (*Precipitation* is the general name given to any kind of water falling from a cloud and includes drizzle, rain, hail, sleet, and every type of snow.)

Air may be relatively moist or dry. Clouds cannot form in very dry air, but the amount of moisture in the air varies widely from place to place and time to time. Water vapor is a gas, of course, and you cannot see it, but the amount present can be measured; this is the *humidity* of the air. In a polar desert, where it is so cold that water vapor changes directly into ice, there may be almost no water vapor in the air, but in warm, moist air it may account for as much as 7% of the air by weight.

Expressed in this way, as the mass of water vapor in a given mass of air, the result is known as the *mixing ratio* or *absolute humidity*. If it is measured as the mass of water vapor in a given mass of air, as a percentage of the largest amount of water vapor the air could hold at that temperature, it is called the *specific humidity*. The term most commonly used, though, is *relative humidity*. When weather forecasters state the humidity, relative humidity is what they mean. When the relative humidity reaches 100%, the air is saturated and water will start to condense.

For water vapor to condense into droplets the air must be cooled until its relative humidity reaches 100%, a temperature known as its *dew point*. Tiny particles must also be present onto which the vapor can condense. As the water condenses, however, something else happens. Condensation releases heat known as *latent heat*. This warms the surrounding air, sometimes enough to make it rise

How clouds are classified

There is an internationally agreed upon scheme for classifying clouds on the basis of their appearance and structure. Under the scheme, clouds are grouped into 10 distinctive types, called *genera* (singular *genus*). The genera are subdivided into *species* (singular and plural) and species into *varieties*. Genera and species names, which are in Latin, have standard abbreviations; variety names are usually written in full. Stratocumulus (Sc), for example, may form in an almond or lens shape, producing the species lenticularis (len), abbreviated as Sc_{len}. If a cloud appears to consist of bands, it may be given the variety name radiatus.

Cloud genera are described as *low-level*, *medium-level*, or *high-level* according to the height at which they most commonly form, although clouds can form at higher or lower levels. Large storm clouds, which have a low-level base but extend to a great height, are counted as low-level clouds, mainly for convenience. Most medium-level clouds have names beginning with the prefix *alto-*, and the names of high-level clouds have the prefix *cirr-*.

Cloud Genera

Low-level clouds. Cloud base from sea level to 1.2 miles.

Stratus (St). An extensive sheet of featureless cloud that will produce drizzle or fine snow if it is thick enough.

Stratocumulus (Sc). Similar to St, but broken into separate, fluffy-looking masses. If thick enough, it also produces drizzle or fine snow.

Cumulus (Cu). Separate, white, fluffy clouds, usually with flat bases. There may be many of them, all with bases at about the same height.

Cumulonimbus (Cb). Very large Cu, often towering to a great height. Because they are so thick, Cb clouds are often dark at the base. If the tops are high enough they will consist of ice crystals and may be swept into an anvil shape. This cloud produces thunderstorms and hailstorms.

Medium-level clouds. Cloud base from 1.2–2.5 miles in polar regions, 1.2 to 4 or 5 miles in temperate and tropical regions.

Altocumulus (Ac). Patches or rolls of cloud joined to make a sheet. Ac is sometimes called *wool-pack cloud*.

Altostratus (As). Pale, watery, featureless cloud that forms a sheet through which the Sun may be visible as a white smudge.

Nimbostratus (Ns). A large sheet of featureless cloud, often with rain or snow, that is thick enough to completely obscure the Sun, Moon, and stars. It makes days dull and nights very dark.

High-level cloud. Cloud base from 2–5 miles in polar regions, 3–11 miles in temperate and tropical regions. All high-level clouds are made entirely from ice crystals.

Cirrus (Ci). Patches of white, fibrous cloud, sometimes swept into strands with curling tails ("mares' tails").

Cirrocumulus (Cc). Patches of thin cloud, sometimes forming ripples, fibrous in places, and with no shading that would define their shape.

Cirrostratus (Cs). Thin, almost transparent cloud forming an extensive sheet and just thick enough to produce a halo around the Sun or Moon.

(Opposite) *Cloud types.*

Latent heat and dew point

Water can exist in three different states, or phases: gas (water vapor), liquid (water), or solid (ice). In the gaseous phase, molecules are free to move in all directions. In the liquid phase, molecules join together in short "strings." In the solid phase, molecules form a closed structure with a space at the center. As water cools, its molecules move closer together and the liquid becomes denser. Pure water at sea-level pressure reaches its densest at 39° F. Below this temperature, the molecules start forming ice crystals. Because these have a space at the center, ice is less dense than water and, weight for weight, has a greater volume. That is why water expands when it freezes and why ice floats on the surface of water.

Molecules bond to one another in the liquid and solid states by the attraction of opposite charges, and energy must be supplied to break those bonds. This energy is absorbed by the molecules without changing their temperature, and the same amount of energy is released when the bonds form again. This is called *latent heat*. For pure water, 600 calories of energy are absorbed to change one gram (1 g = 0.035 oz.) from liquid to gas (evaporation) and 80 calories to melt one gram of ice. Sublimation, the direct change from ice to vapor without passing through the liquid phase, absorbs 680 calories for each gram (the sum of the latent heats of melting and evaporation). In each case, the same amount of energy is released when water vapor condenses into liquid water and when water freezes.

Energy to supply the latent heat is taken from the surrounding air or water. When ice melts or water evaporates, the air and water in

Latent heat.

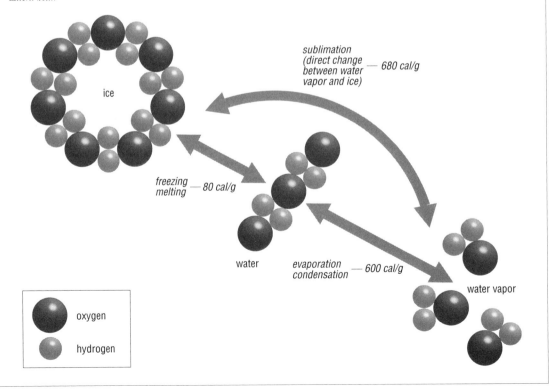

contact with them are cooled, because energy has been taken from them. That is why it often feels cold during a thaw and why our bodies can cool themselves by sweating and allowing the sweat to evaporate.

When latent heat is released by freezing and condensation, the surroundings are warmed. This is very important in the formation of the storm clouds from which hurricanes and tornadoes develop. Warm air rises, its water vapor condenses, and this warms the air still more, making it rise higher.

Warm air can hold more water vapor than cool air. If moist air is cooled, its water vapor will condense into liquid droplets. The temperature at which this occurs is called the *dew point*. It is the temperature at which dew forms on surfaces and evaporates from them.

At the dew point temperature, the air is saturated with water vapor. The amount of moisture in the air is usually expressed as its *relative humidity*. This is the amount of water present as a percentage of the amount needed to saturate the air at that temperature.

to a higher level, displacing the denser air above it, which sinks and warms adiabatically, sometimes enough to evaporate the water droplets in it. Evaporation absorbs latent heat from the surrounding air, cooling it, and this may cause the air to sink even further. If you have ever flown through a cloud, in an airplane, you will know that it looks just like fog and gives the impression of being nothing more than a great mass of very tiny water droplets hanging motionless in

Figure 7: *Electrostatic charge inside a storm cloud.*

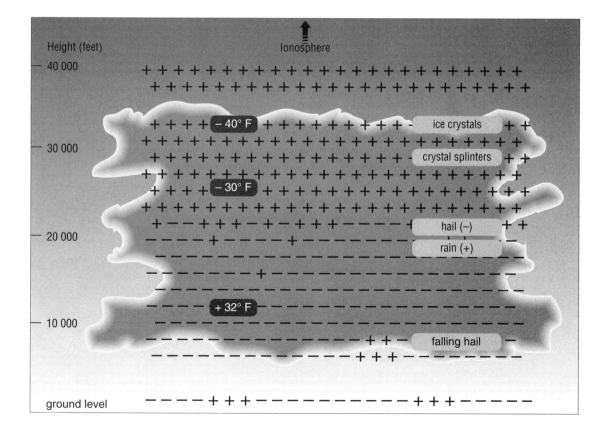

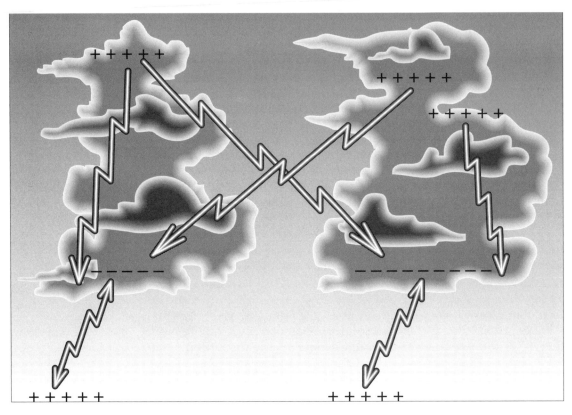

Figure 8: *Electrical charge and lightning.*

the air. In fact, though, very complicated things are going on inside any cloud (see box on page 26).

In highly unstable air, conditions inside a cloud can be extremely violent. If you have ever flown through or even close to cumuliform (heaped) clouds, you may have been advised to fasten your seat belt because the air is likely to be "bumpy" due to the strong vertical air currents that alternately lift the airplane upwards and then drop it again. It is not very likely that you will have flown through a real storm cloud. Pilots avoid them, and for good reason. The electrical fields inside them can make compasses and other instruments useless, and the vertical air currents can make the airplane uncontrollable or even tear it apart.

Inside a storm cloud, air is rising by convection and cooling adiabatically. At a certain height known as the *condensation level*, air cools to its dew point and water droplets start to form. This level marks the base of the cloud. The air is still rising strongly, and the release of latent heat warms it and makes it rise even faster. It is mainly the release of the latent heat of condensation in the towering clouds that form in very warm, very moist air that drives the low-latitude Hadley cells.

Eventually, the rising air cools so much that its water droplets freeze, releasing still more latent heat. As they grow larger and heavier, ice crystals start to fall, colliding with one another and splintering as they do so. At a lower level they melt, but are then carried aloft again in rising air currents, so droplets freeze, fall to a level at which they start to melt, then freeze again, collecting more water all the time. This is how hailstones form. If you could cut through one you would see it is layered, like an onion. When a hailstone grows too heavy for the upcurrents to lift, it falls from the cloud and the bigger the stones that reach the ground in a hailstorm, the stronger the upcurrents in the cloud above.

Inside the storm cloud, upcurrents and downcurrents form side by side and water is constantly changing from vapor to liquid to ice and back again. Before long this starts to distribute electrical charges inside the cloud. As figure 7 shows, the upper part of the cloud becomes positively charged and the lower part negatively charged.

Electricity flows constantly from the ionosphere to the surface of the Earth. In the ionosphere at a height of about 55–125 miles, molecules absorb enough energy from solar radiation to strip electrons from atomic nuclei. An atom that has lost one or more electrons is an *ion* and is said to have been *ionized*, hence the name *ionosphere*. The electrons, carrying a negative charge, flow downward, leaving the ionized nuclei with a positive charge and the Earth's surface with a negative charge. Inside a storm cloud this electrical polarization becomes much stronger, and the powerful negative charge at the base of the cloud can induce local areas of positive charge on the ground.

Air is a good electrical insulator, but the strength of the electrical field can locally exceed about 300,000 volts per foot. When this happens a spark flies from positive to negative. This is lightning, leaping from place to place wherever the attraction is strongest along a forking path. The lightning spark heats the air around so suddenly the air expands in the explosion we hear as thunder.

As figure 8 shows, lightning will spark from one place in a cloud to another in the same cloud. From the ground this appears as a white flash, or *sheet lightning*. It can also spark from one cloud to another and, of course, between a cloud and the ground. In this case, however, the first spark actually travels upward, from the positively charged surface to the negatively charged cloud base. This relatively inconspicuous flash immediately causes a much bigger return flash, from cloud to ground, which is the one we notice. The spark itself is only an inch or so in diameter, but it carries a current of about 10,000 amperes. That is enough electricity to power about 350 small electric space heaters — but only for a fraction of a second.

Thunderstorms can develop only in very large, towering clouds. Often they extend from a height of 1,000 feet or so all the way to the tropopause. This much height is needed for water to exist as

Evaporation, condensation, and the formation of clouds

When air rises it cools adiabatically, by an average of 3.5° F every 1,000 feet. This is called the *dry adiabatic lapse rate*. Moving air may be forced to rise if it crosses high ground, such as a mountain or mountain range, or meets a mass of cooler, denser air at a front. Locally, air may also rise by convection where the ground is warmed unevenly.

There will be a height, called the *condensation level*, at which the temperature of the air falls to its dew point. As the air rises above this level the water vapor it contains will start to condense. Condensation releases latent heat, warming the air. After the relative humidity of the air reaches 100% and the air continues to rise, it will cool at the saturated adiabatic lapse rate of about 3° F per 1,000 feet.

Water vapor will condense at a relative humidity as low as 78% if the air contains minute particles of a substance that readily dissolves in water. Salt crystals and sulfate particles are common examples. Such substances readily take up water molecules from the air and become droplets of a concentrated solution. Water evaporates much more slowly from a solution than from pure water, so the droplets survive longer and grow by gathering more water molecules. If the air contains insoluble particles, such as dust, the vapor will condense at about 100% relative humidity. If there are no particles at all, the relative humidity may exceed 100% and the air will be supersaturated, although the relative humidity in clouds rarely exceeds 101%.

The particles onto which water vapor condenses are called *cloud condensation nuclei* (CCN). They range in size from 0.001 μm to more than 10 μm in diameter; water will condense onto the smallest particles only if the air is strongly supersaturated, and the largest particles are so heavy they do not remain airborne very long. Condensation is most efficient on CCN averaging 0.2 μm diameter (1 μm = one-millionth of a meter = 0.00004 inches).

At first, water droplets vary in size according to the size of the nuclei onto which they condensed. After that, the droplets grow but also lose water by evaporation because they are warmed by the latent heat of condensation. Some freeze, grow into snowflakes, and then melt as they fall into a lower, warmer region of the cloud. Others grow as large droplets collide and merge with smaller ones.

Cloud formation.

1) *forced to rise over high ground (orographic lifting)*
2) *convection due to uneven heating of the ground*
3) *forced to rise along a front*

liquid in some places and ice at others and to produce strong vertical currents. Such (cumulonimbus) clouds form in unstable air or in air that becomes unstable once something has forced it to start rising.

There are several ways in which air can be made to rise. These account for the formation of most clouds of the cumuliform (heaped) type (see box on page 24), including most cumulonimbus thunderstorm clouds. Over the tropical seas, however, the convective forces inside a weather system that produces cumulonimbus may sometimes be so strong that the system as a whole becomes much more violent than even the largest thunderstorm. It may grow into a tropical storm and then into a full hurricane.

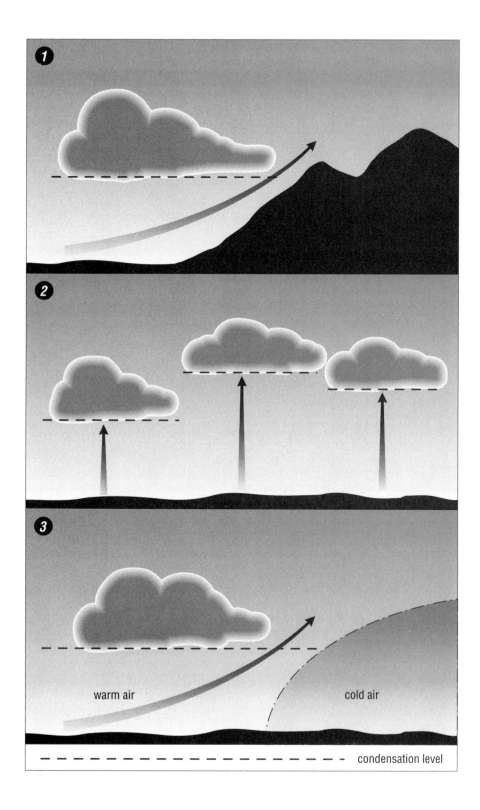

warm air

cold air

- condensation level

Figure 9: *Cumulonimbus cloud.*
(National Center for Atmospheric
Research/National Science Foundation)

How a hurricane begins

Where the trade winds meet, there is a permanent area of low pressure called the *equatorial trough*. This is where winds from the northeast in the northern hemisphere and southeast in the southern hemisphere converge and air rises strongly. The trough moves north and south with the seasons, but in a very complicated way that scientists do not fully understand. Hurricanes form either along the equatorial trough or close to it but not directly over the equator, because the Coriolis effect is nonexistent there.

Hurricanes form only over very warm water. The sea-surface temperature must be at least 80° F over a large area. This means hurricanes can begin only in the tropics in summer. Air in contact with the sea is warmed by it, expanding and rising more than surrounding air, and so an area of low atmospheric pressure develops. Although the water is warm, it is only slightly warmer than the sea everywhere else in the same latitude. The tropics receive so much solar energy that air moves very quickly and temperatures and pressures are much the same throughout the region.

Nevertheless, local areas of slightly warmer and lower pressure are common. Some are caused where the southern trade winds are stronger than elsewhere and push a section of the equatorial trough northward, forming a wave or "kink" in it. Others begin as tropical thunderstorms over land and then move westward. These are called *easterly waves* or *tropical waves* and, as figure 10 shows, they "bend" the trade winds. At first they are strong enough to cause only thunderstorms. If they persist for several days they are known as *tropical disturbances*. Most are harmless, but a few strengthen as they move west, growing into tropical depressions, with winds up to 38 MPH, then into tropical storms, with winds up to 73 MPH. Now and again one will grow further, into a full-scale hurricane.

For a tropical disturbance to grow, air must be rising within it very vigorously. In the tropics, warm air is rising high into the atmosphere, cooling, sinking, and returning toward the equator as the trade winds. It begins to sink as soon as it reaches its maximum height and starts to cool. As it sinks it warms adiabatically. This produces a layer of high-level air that is warmer than the air below it, called a *high-level temperature inversion*. Ordinarily, rising warm air is trapped beneath it and this limits the height to which storm clouds can grow. If they are growing very vigorously, however, driven by unusually strong upcurrents, they may penetrate the high-level inversion. When this happens the clouds become towering giants up to 40,000 feet tall, producing the fierce storms of a tropical depression.

If a tropical storm is to grow still further into a hurricane, the low pressure at the surface must be accompanied by high pressure at

Figure 10: *Development of a tropical storm.*

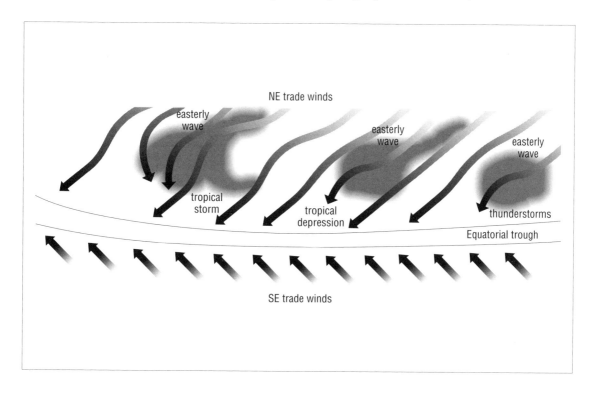

Christoph Buys Ballot and his law

In 1857, the Dutch meteorologist Christoph Buys Ballot (see volume 6 for a biographical note) published a summary of his observations on the relationship between atmospheric pressure and wind. He had concluded that in the northern hemisphere winds flow counterclockwise around areas of low pressure and clockwise around areas of high pressure. In the southern hemisphere these directions are reversed.

Unknown to Buys Ballot, a few months earlier the American meteorologist William Ferrel had applied the laws of physics and calculated this would be the case. Buys Ballot

Buys Ballot's law.
In the northern hemisphere winds flow in a clockwise direction around centers of high pressure and counterclockwise around centers of low pressure. Therefore, if you stand with your back to the wind the center of low pressure is to your left. In the southern hemisphere these directions are reversed.

acknowledged Ferrel's prior claim to the discovery, but despite this, the phenomenon is now known as *Buys Ballot's law*. This states that, in the northern hemisphere, if you stand with your back to the wind the area of low pressure is to your left and the area of high pressure to your right. In the southern hemisphere, if you stand with your back to the wind the area of low pressure is to your right and the area of high pressure to your left. (The law does not apply very close to the equator.)

The law is a consequence of the combined effect of the *pressure-gradient force* (PGF) and the *Coriolis effect* or *Coriolis force* (CorF). Air flows from an area of high pressure to one of low pressure, like water flowing downhill. Just as the speed of flowing water depends on the steepness of the slope (the gradient), so the speed of flowing air depends on the difference in pressure between high and low (the PGF).

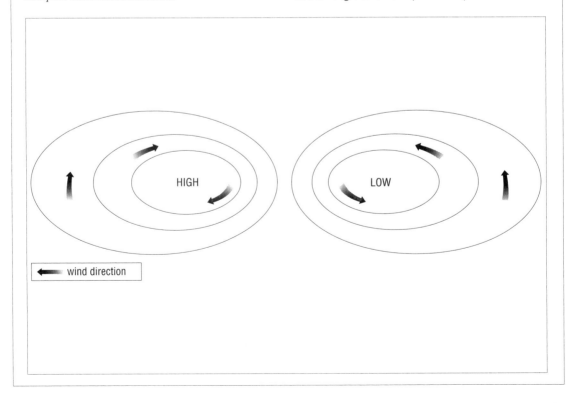

HIGH

LOW

◀━━ wind direction

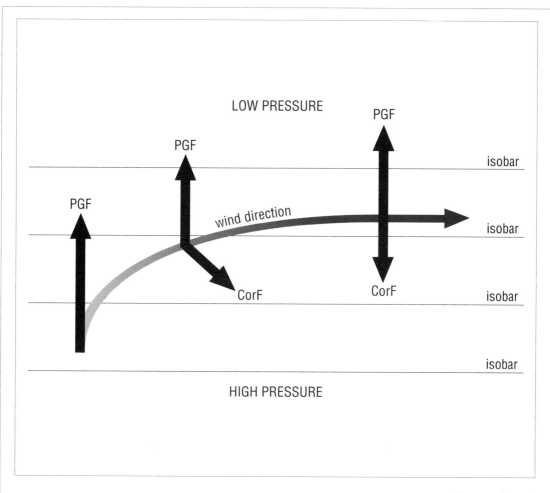

The geostrophic wind.

As the air flows, the CorF, acting at right angles to the direction of flow, swings it to the right in the northern hemisphere and to the left in the southern hemisphere. As it starts to swing to the right, the CorF and PGF produce a resultant force which accelerates it. CorF is proportional to the speed of the moving air, so it increases, swinging the air still more to the right. This continues until the air is flowing parallel to the isobars (at right angles to the pressure gradient). At this point, the PGF and CorF are acting in opposite directions. If the PGF is the stronger force, the air will swing to the left and accelerate. This will increase the CorF, swinging it back to the right again. If the CorF is the stronger, the air will swing further to the right, the PGF acting in the opposite direction will slow it, the CorF will decrease, and the air will swing to the left again. The eventual result is to make the air flow parallel to the isobars (pressure gradient) rather than across them.

Near the ground, friction with the surface and objects on it slow the air, acting as an additional force. This deflects the air so it flows at an angle to the isobars, rather than parallel to them. Clear of the surface, the air does flow parallel to the isobars. This is called the *geostrophic wind*.

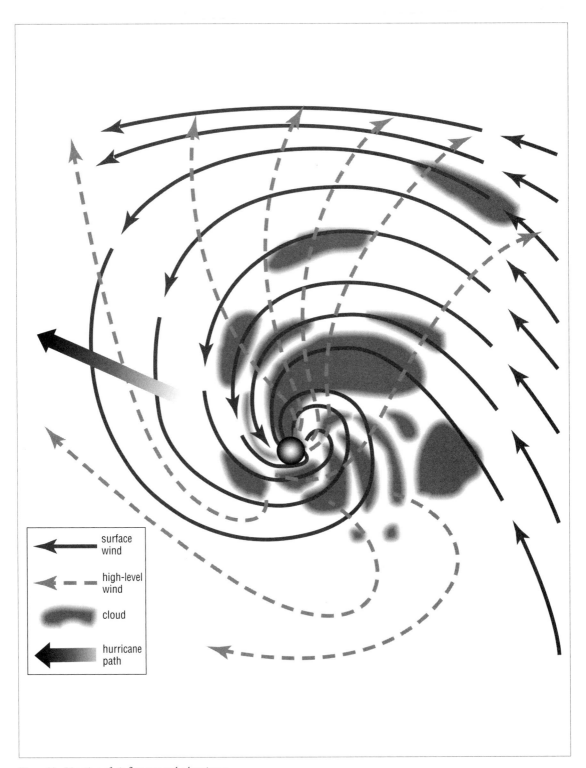

Figure 11: *Direction of air flow around a hurricane.*

an altitude of about 56,000 feet, near the tropopause. This high pressure, called an *anticyclone*, may be the remains of an earlier weather system or it may be produced by the rising air of the low-pressure system (called a *cyclone*) below. In either case, the strong vertical movement of air will intensify the anticyclone by constantly feeding air into it.

Air flows from an area of high pressure to one of low pressure, but not in a straight line. Influenced by the Coriolis effect (see box on page 40), the air swings to the right until it flows around the high- or low-pressure area. In the northern hemisphere, air circulates clockwise around areas of high pressure and counterclockwise around areas of low pressure (these directions are reversed in the southern hemisphere). This was discovered in 1857 by the Dutch meteorologist Christoph Buys Ballot and is known as *Buys Ballot's law* (see box on page 34).

Air drawn into the low-pressure area near the surface flows around it counterclockwise (in the northern hemisphere). This is called *cyclonic circulation*. The wind strengthens until the difference in pressure between the high- and low-pressure areas can accelerate it no further. Then it rises, spiraling upward until it meets the upper-level anticyclone. There, the circulation is clockwise (anticyclonic) and it sweeps the rising air outwards, away from the center (see figure 11).

Alternatively, air may be swept away at high levels if the surface low-pressure area forms near the subtropical *jet stream*, but not directly beneath it. Jet streams are upper-level winds, blowing from west to east in both hemispheres, that occur at the boundary between bodies of air at markedly different temperatures. The subtropical jet stream is associated with the meeting of tropical and midlatitude air, usually around latitude 30°, and it can blow at 100 MPH or more, the wind speed being proportional to the difference in temperature of the air to either side. The jet stream is farther from the equator in summer than in winter, but waves develop in it, some of which may take it deep into the tropics. Should a tropical depression intensify close to it, the jet stream will carry away upper-level air and have an effect similar to that of an upper-level anticyclone.

By removing the rising air, the anticyclone or jet stream draws more air upward. This makes the surface atmospheric pressure fall still further (although directly below the jet stream, air is removed so quickly that surface pressure remains too high for a hurricane to form). The pressure drop is not great; ordinarily, the average sea-level pressure is 1,016 millibars (mb), while at the center of a hurricane it is generally between 920 mb and 980 mb. This is a drop of only 4–10%, but it is enough.

Now there is an area of low surface pressure, 400 miles or more across, in which huge storm clouds have developed. Warm, moist air, drawn toward the center, circulates cyclonically and in an upward spiral all the way to the cloud tops then disperses outward, drawing more air from below. While it remains a tropical depression, there is cold air at the center with warmer air circulating around it. There are rain showers at the center and the sky is mainly overcast. When the air in the center becomes warmer than the air flowing around it, the sky clears until only a few small clouds remain, there is no rain, and the wind speed falls to about 10 MPH. This calm center, often 20 to 30 miles across, is surrounded by what looks like a solid wall of cloud. It is the "eye" of what has now grown into a hurricane.

Vortices

When you pull the plug from a full bathtub and the water starts flowing away, after a little while it will begin to swirl in a spiral, forming a little whirlpool. If you watch the water each time you do this and note the direction in which it turns, you will find that sometimes it turns to the right and sometimes to the left. If, while it is swirling, you churn up the water and break up the whirlpool, then leave it to start swirling again, it may turn in the opposite direction to the one in which it turned earlier. The direction it turns is a matter of chance. Some people will tell you that the water always flows counterclockwise in the northern hemisphere and that if you cross the equator and take a bath there, it will flow clockwise. This is a popular belief and difficult to dislodge, but it is wrong. It mixes up two physical effects.

On the small scale of a bathtub, moving water is affected by *vorticity*. This is the tendency of any moving fluid, liquid or gas, to begin turning about an axis and it is what produces the whirlpool, or *vortex*. The axis may be horizontal or vertical. In the case of the bathtub, where the water is flowing downwards, the axis is at right angles to the Earth's surface. Air is also a fluid and when it moves it also develops vorticity, and its vorticity about a vertical axis contributes greatly to the development of a hurricane.

Vorticity begins when two streams of water or wind flow side by side in the same direction but at different speeds. The faster is slowed on one side by the slower, and this makes it start to curve towards the slower. You use this effect to help you steer a rowboat. To make the boat turn, you row more strongly with one oar than with the other, and the boat follows a path that curves toward the side where you are rowing more slowly.

Imagine a body that is spinning around its own axis. You can measure its mass, the radius of the circle it describes, and the speed of its rotation, which is called its *angular velocity* and is measured as the number of degrees through which it turns in a given time. Multiply these together and the product, called *angular momentum*, is a constant. Call the mass *M*, the radius *R*, and the angular velocity *V*, and $M \times R \times V$ = a constant. *M*, *R*, and *V* are variables. They can alter, but their product is a constant and must remain the same.

This is called the *conservation of angular momentum* and it means that if one of the variables changes, one or two of the others will also change so the constant remains the same. Dancers and ice skaters make use of this when they perform pirouettes. The dancer starts spinning with her arms fully outstretched. The distance from the center of her body (the axis of her rotation) to her fingertips is the diameter of the circle her body describes; the radius is half of this. Then she slowly draws her arms inward to her body. This reduces her radius of spin. In figure 12, her fingertips begin by describing the outer circle, and when she has withdrawn her arms she describes the inner circle.

Her mass cannot change (she cannot suddenly become heavier) and so the remaining variable, her angular velocity, changes. It increases as her radius of spin decreases. In other words, she spins

Figure 12: *Conservation of angular momentum.*

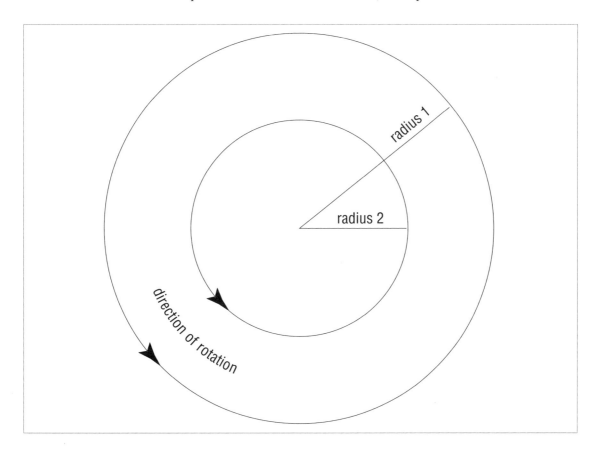

The Coriolis effect

Any object moving towards or away from the equator and not firmly attached to the surface does not travel in a straight line. It is deflected to the right in the northern hemisphere and to the left in the southern hemisphere. Moving air and water tend to follow a clockwise path in the northern hemisphere and a counterclockwise path in the southern hemisphere.

The reason for this was discovered in 1835 by the French physicist Gaspard Gustave de Coriolis and it is called the *Coriolis effect*. It happens because the Earth is a rotating sphere and as an object moves above the surface, the Earth below is also moving. The effect used to be called the Coriolis *force*, but it is not a force. It results simply from the fact that we observe motion in relation to fixed points on the surface. The effect is easily demonstrated by the simple experiment described in volume 6.

The Earth makes one complete turn on its axis every 24 hours. This means every point on the surface is constantly moving and returns to its original position (relative to the Sun) every 24 hours, but different points on the surface travel different distances to do so. Consider two points on the surface, one at the equator and the other at 40° N, which is the approximate latitude of New York and Madrid. The equator, latitude 0°, is about 24,881 miles long. That is how far a point on the equator must travel in 24 hours, which means it moves at about 1,037 MPH. At 40° N, the circumference parallel to the equator is about 19,057 miles. The point there has less distance to travel and so it moves at about 794 MPH.

The Coriolis effect.

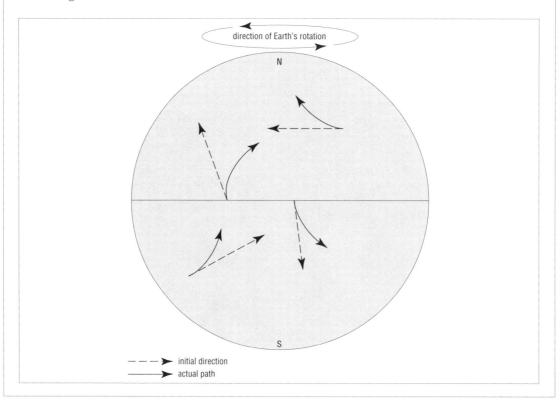

direction of Earth's rotation

N

S

— — — ▶ initial direction
———————▶ actual path

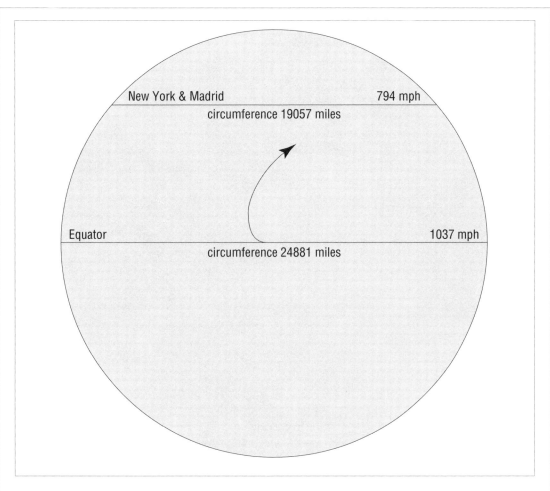

New York & Madrid 794 mph
circumference 19057 miles

Equator 1037 mph
circumference 24881 miles

Suppose you planned to fly an aircraft to New York from the point on the equator due south of New York (and could ignore the winds). If you headed due north you would not reach New York. At the equator you are already traveling eastward at 1,037 MPH. As you fly north, you will continue to move eastward at your initial, equatorial speed. The surface beneath you is also traveling east, but at a slower speed the further you travel. If the journey from 0° to 40° N took you six hours, in that time you would also move about 6,000 miles to the east relative to the position of the surface beneath you, but the surface itself would also move, at New York by about 4,700 miles, so you would end not at New York, but

The Coriolis effect.
The Coriolis effect deflects air masses and winds to the right in the northern hemisphere and to the left in the southern hemisphere. It has no effect at the equator and maximum effect at the poles.

(6,000 - 4,700 =) 1,300 miles to the east of New York, way out over the Atlantic.

The size of the Coriolis effect is directly proportional to the speed at which the body moves and its latitude. The effect on a body moving at 100 MPH is ten times greater than that on one moving at 10 MPH, and the Coriolis effect is greatest at the poles and zero at the equator.

faster. You may not be able to perform a pirouette yourself, but you can demonstrate the conservation of angular momentum quite simply (see the experiment in volume 6).

When air moves, vorticity causes it to swing until it moves in a circle. If that circle becomes smaller, the conservation of its angular momentum will make the air move faster. Around a hurricane, where air is spiraling inward, the wind speed increases the closer it is to the central eye.

If the turning air moves in a clockwise direction it is said to have *negative vorticity* and if it turns counterclockwise it is said to have *positive vorticity.* A counterclockwise air flow is also called *cyclonic* (and a clockwise flow *anticyclonic*) because these are the directions of the wind around areas of low (cyclones) and high (anticyclones) pressure. Buys Ballot's law describes this kind of air movement and the reason for it is explained in the box on page 34.

It is this effect that leads people to suppose that in the northern hemisphere water leaving a bathtub will invariably spiral clockwise around the low pressure at the center of the whirlpool. This does not happen, but not because the effect is unreal. It is real enough, but it applies only to masses of air or water very much bigger than the contents of a bathtub and that are moving across the surface of the Earth.

When we observe air movements we do so from a fixed position, standing (or sitting) in a particular place. It is easy to forget that the Earth itself is rotating and we are traveling with it. Air also travels with the Earth, but it is not attached firmly to the surface and so it may be traveling at a different speed. Indeed, if it moves from one latitude to another it will start by traveling at much the same speed as the surface in its first latitude and this speed will be different from the speed the surface is moving in its new latitude, so then it is bound to be traveling at a different speed from the surface.

People realized long ago that the rotation of the Earth affects the way air moves over its surface, but it was not until 1835 that the French engineer Gaspard Gustave de Coriolis found out why. Today this is known as the *Coriolis effect* (see box on page 40). Its strength ranges from zero at the equator to a maximum at the poles and it is vorticity, not the Coriolis effect, that deflects the equatorial trade winds, making them flow from an easterly direction rather than from due north and south.

Vorticity accounts for the ferocity of the winds around the eye of a hurricane and the Coriolis effect explains the direction in which those winds blow. The Coriolis effect also explains why hurricanes cannot form fewer than 5° N or S of the equator and why it contributes to the path they follow once they have formed.

What happens inside a hurricane

As air flows in from surrounding regions of higher atmospheric pressure to fill the deepening tropical depression and the system starts rotating, a distinct structure begins to develop. By the time the tropical depression has grown into a tropical storm and then into a hurricane, it is this structure that sustains its force.

Its energy is immense. If all of it could be converted into electricity, in two days an average hurricane could release enough heat energy to supply the whole of the United States for a year. That is about three million kilowatt-hours (one kilowatt-hour is the energy used in an hour by one bar of an ordinary electric fire). It is also equivalent to the explosive energy of about 400 hydrogen bombs of 20 megatons each (a megaton is the power of one million tons of conventional high explosive).

The Coriolis effect swings moving air around the low-pressure area, but this is countered by friction between the wind and sea. Friction slows the wind, reducing the Coriolis effect (which is proportional to wind speed), so the pressure-gradient force is slightly greater than the Coriolis effect and the wind spirals inward to the low-pressure area. Friction with the sea also produces vast quantities of spray. Droplets of sea water evaporate in the warm air, adding to the water evaporated from the sea surface.

Spiraling inward, the air is warmed by contact with the sea. This makes it expand and rise. The air is moist to a considerable height

Figure 13: *Cross section of a hurricane.*

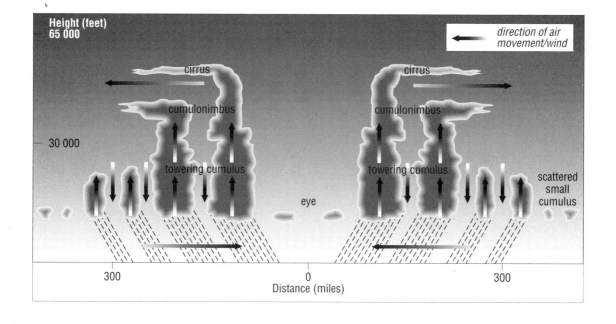

because of the large amounts of water that evaporate into it over the tropical ocean and the addition of spray. The rising air cools adiabatically (see box on page 16) and its water vapor starts to condense. Condensation releases latent heat, warming the air again and making it continue to rise. Still spiraling inward and moving with increasing speed as it approaches the center, because of the partial conservation of its angular momentum, the air continues to rise and its water vapor continues to condense.

This vigorous convection, with upcurrents rising at up to 30 MPH, produces cumulonimbus (storm) clouds that sometimes tower to a height of 50,000 feet. Violent thunderstorms develop and beneath the clouds the rainfall is torrential and often accompanied by hail.

Wind speeds fall off rapidly near the top until the air is moving more slowly than the rotating surface of the Earth, and again because of the Coriolis effect, they begin to move anticyclonically (clockwise in the northern hemisphere), producing the wide, curving trails of cloud that make a hurricane photographed from space look very like a spiral galaxy. This anticyclonic circulation carries away and disperses much of the rising air, but not quite all of it. Some sinks again from the high-level region of high pressure. It descends at the center of the vortex, warming adiabatically as it does so. Its rising temperature increases its water-holding capacity. If fragments of the surrounding cloud are swept into it, most of the water droplets in them evaporate. The warm air produces the almost clear skies and warmth at the eye of the hurricane. The warmth is very noticeable and after the raging wind and rain has passed, the comparatively still air at the eye, several degrees warmer than the air outside the hurricane, can seem oppressive.

In the middle and upper regions of the storm, there is a large difference in temperature between the air inside the eye and that outside it. This produces a correspondingly large difference in air pressure, adding to the energy of the hurricane.

Despite the sinking air, it is in the eye that the surface atmospheric pressure is at its lowest. It is often more than 50 millibars lower than the pressure outside the hurricane. The most severe category of hurricanes have a pressure of 920 mb or less. Taking the average sea-level pressure as 1,016 mb, this is a drop of 96 mb, and as a hurricane approaches, atmospheric pressure may fall at a rate of 3 mb per mile. If the storm travels at, say, 20 MPH, this means the pressure will fall about 1 mb every minute. Reduced pressure in the eye means a smaller weight of air is pressing down on the surface of the sea. This allows the sea surface to rise up to three feet higher than the surrounding sea level. The power of a hurricane is often measured by comparing the temperature and pressure in the eye with those beyond the influence of the system.

The outward flow of air (called *divergence*) at the top of the storm increases the inward flow (*convergence*) near the surface. This intensifies the winds and, therefore, strengthens the upward spiral, which leads in turn to the condensation of water vapor and release of latent heat, and the rising air adds to that already at the top, sustaining the high pressure. At this stage the storm is feeding on itself and it will continue to do so for as long as it has an ample supply of water and is being warmed from below.

Towering cumulonimbus clouds form a circle surrounding the eye and extending almost from sea level all the way to the tropopause. This is the dark *eyewall* of the hurricane, often with tattered fragments of cloud falling down its face, and it is where conditions are most severe. As figure 13 shows, at the top of the eyewall, the remaining water vapor in the air carried away by divergence freezes to form cirrus and cirrostratus clouds, made from ice crystals. In satellite photographs of hurricanes, these thin, high-level clouds often show clearly, spiraling out from the edge of the main cloud mass.

In all, there may be up to 200 towers of cumulonimbus, which form in bands. Outside the eyewall cloud there is a cloud-free band. This is surrounded in its turn by a second circular band of cloud, then another cloud-free band, and further alternating bands of cloud and clear air, with the clouds becoming smaller the farther they are from the center. At any one time, it will be raining or hailing in about 15% of the area covered by bands of cloud. The weather is dry in the cloud-free bands, but the sky is not blue. Divergence at the top of the storm spreads enough cloud to cover the sky.

Within the area of the hurricane, often more than 400 miles across, the *cloud towers* cover no more than about 1% of the surface, yet they form the heart of the storm by releasing so much latent heat and producing the warm center without which a hurricane cannot develop. In the cloud-free bands between the cloud bands, some of the air carried aloft is descending, warming adiabatically, and feeding back into the system at the surface.

Rain, hail, and thunderstorms are relatively common. Think of a hurricane, though, and the image that springs to mind is of the wind, which is this storm's most important and obvious characteristic.

Wind force is still measured by a scale devised at the beginning of the 19th century by a British admiral (see box on page 46). In the days of sailing ships, the Royal Navy thought it advisable to supply British sailors with a simple method for estimating the strength of the wind so they could know how much sail to set. A sailing ship could be severely damaged or even sunk if it carried too much sail for the wind conditions and in those days ships did not have instruments (called anemometers) for measuring wind speed. Even if they had, it is doubtful whether an ordinary anemometer could have withstood winds of hurricane force.

The Beaufort scale is straightforward and easy for anyone to use. You need only look from your window to estimate the Beaufort wind

Wind force and Admiral Beaufort

In 1806, the Royal Navy issued a scale by which sailors could estimate the strength of the wind by observing its effects. The scale also instructed them on the amount of sail appropriate to each wind strength.

The scale had been devised by Admiral Sir Francis Beaufort (see volume 6 for a biographical note) and is still known as the Beaufort scale. Eventually it was adopted internationally.

The Beaufort scale classifies winds into 13 named *forces* (in 1955 meteorologists at the United States Weather Bureau added five more to describe hurricane-force winds). Wind speeds were originally given in knots, the unit still often used by ships and aircraft. In the scale given here, knots have been converted to miles per hour and rounded to the nearest whole number. (1 knot = 1 nautical mile per hour = 1.15 MPH.)

Force 0.   1 MPH or less. Calm. The air feels still and smoke rises vertically.

Force 1.   1–3 MPH. Light air. Wind vanes and flags do not move, but rising smoke drifts.

Force 2.   4–7 MPH. Light breeze. Drifting smoke indicates the wind direction.

Force 3.   8–12 MPH. Gentle breeze. Leaves rustle, small twigs move, and flags made from lightweight material stir gently.

Force 4.   13–18 MPH. Moderate breeze. Loose leaves and pieces of paper blow about.

Force 5.   19–24 MPH. Fresh breeze. Small trees that are in full leaf wave in the wind.

Force 6.   25–31 MPH. Strong breeze. It becomes difficult to use an open umbrella.

Force 7.   32–38 MPH. Moderate gale. The wind exerts strong pressure on people walking into it.

Force 8.   39–46 MPH. Fresh gale. Small twigs are torn from trees.

Force 9.   47–54 MPH. Strong gale. Chimneys blown down, slates and tiles torn from roofs.

Force 10.   55–63 MPH. Whole gale. Trees are broken or uprooted.

Force 11.   64–75 MPH. Storm. Trees are uprooted and blown some distance. Cars are overturned.

Force 12.   More than 75 MPH. Hurricane. Devastation is widespread. Buildings are destroyed, many trees uprooted. In the original instruction, "no sail can stand."

force. That is its great advantage. Its disadvantage is that it classes any wind stronger than 75 MPH as a hurricane (force 12) and 75 MPH is the minimum wind speed for a hurricane. If the wind speed is less than 75 MPH it is not a hurricane at all, and in the most severe hurricanes it is more than 155 MPH. For this reason, the United States Weather Bureau has added a further five categories to describe hurricanes with winds from 75 MPH, called category 1, to category 5, with winds of more than 155 MPH (see the box on page 85).

At sea, the winds raise huge waves, then whip away their tops, so it becomes impossible to see where the sea ends and the sky begins. The wind speed is not constant. Like most winds, a hurricane produces gusts much stronger than the main wind. A wind of 110 MPH will raise 30-foot waves, and most hurricanes can produce gusts much stronger than this. Not even the largest ships sail through such a storm deliberately, but occasionally they do so by accident.

In 1944, a U.S. battle fleet in the Philippine Sea was misinformed about the location and movement of a small but extremely violent typhoon (the name given to a hurricane in that part of the world) and sailed directly toward its center. Sailors know, from Buys Ballot's law, that in the northern hemisphere, if they stand with their backs to the wind, the storm center will be to the left. In this case, however, the meteorological officer was confident he knew exactly where the storm was and that it was moving away from the fleet. By the time the commanding admiral realized the mistake it was too late. His ships were sailing into the storm rather than away from it, and already they were struggling through 70-foot waves and winds of more than 115 MPH. By the time the fleet was clear, three destroyers had sunk, 146 aircraft were destroyed on board carriers, the remaining ships were too severely damaged to continue with their mission, and 790 sailors had been lost.

If a ship has no choice but to sail close to a hurricane, it is safer to pass on the side of its path nearest to the equator. There, the counterclockwise winds will blow the ship behind the storm. The winds on the other side, which are in any case stronger because they blow in the same direction as that in which the storm is moving, will carry the ship in front of the storm, with a serious risk of being drawn into it.

Waves generated by the wind move outward from the center of the storm. As the storm moves, it continues to produce waves. These mix with earlier waves, but the movement of the hurricane means the direction of the waves is changing constantly, so waves may cross one another. The sea looks as though it is boiling, especially behind the eye of the hurricane, and the disturbance affects the sea over vast distances.

With so much energy being released so violently, a hurricane cannot survive for long. Most last no more than two or three days before their wind speeds decrease. A dying hurricane may continue as a deep depression that brings gales strong enough to cause considerable damage; the storm may keep the name it was given during its life as a hurricane, but by this time it is not a hurricane anymore.

The hurricane's structure of concentric circles of cloud around a very warm center allows it to sustain itself during its brief life; that structure results from three conditions which the storm does not produce and over which it has no control:

The sea-surface temperature must be higher than 80° F. Should it fall below 76° F there will be insufficient heat to maintain the convective currents that generate the towering cumulonimbus clouds. As the hurricane moves into a higher latitude it will cross cooler water and lose its source of heat.

There must be abundant water to release latent heat as it condenses. Should the storm move over land, it will lose its supply of water.

Finally, there must be a high-level anticyclone to disperse the rising air and thereby draw more air from below. The anticyclone may weaken, or drift away, or the hurricane may move from beneath it.

It is pure coincidence if all three of these necessary conditions are present at the same time and in the same place as a strengthening tropical storm, and the coincidence cannot last. After a few days one or other condition will be lost. The hurricane will weaken, then disappear.

Where hurricanes occur

Hurricanes begin as tropical depressions, areas where the atmospheric pressure is just a little lower than it is in the air surrounding it. They are strictly a tropical phenomenon. It would be impossible for a hurricane to form over Minnesota, for example, or over Europe, although a hurricane traveling from the tropics might reach such places, much weakened during its long journey from its sources of energy.

Hurricanes form in the tropics because it is only there that the necessary conditions ever occur. Figure 14 is a map showing where they form and the directions in which they move from their "breeding grounds."

What we in the western hemisphere call a hurricane goes by different names in other parts of the world. If it forms in the Bay of Bengal it is known as a *cyclone*. Over most of the Pacific it is called a *typhoon*, although near Indonesia it is called a *baguio*. If it occurs near Australia it is a typhoon, but some people call it a *willy-nilly*. All of these storms are the same, despite their different names. Meteorologists call all of them *tropical cyclones*. A cyclone is an area of low atmospheric pressure; its opposite is an *anticyclone*, which is an area of high pressure. As the name suggests, a tropical cyclone is one that forms in the tropics. Like cyclones elsewhere in the world, it is a distinct area of low pressure. In the tropics it becomes much more intense than in higher latitudes, but otherwise it is similar.

For a tropical cyclone to develop, first there must be a fall in atmospheric pressure over a fairly large area. The difference need not be great. A drop of a mere 20 mb over about two days is sufficient, enough to produce only a weak depression. In temperate latitudes such a fall is common, although it is unusual in the tropics, where the air pressure is fairly constant over very large areas. Under certain circumstances this small fall in pressure is enough to trigger the development of a tropical depression from which a hurricane (tropical cyclone) may grow.

It may be that a pocket of low-pressure air becomes detached from the edge of a mid-latitude weather system and spills over into the tropics as a tongue of low pressure (called a *trough*) extending towards the equator at a high altitude. Alternatively, a low-pressure system on land may drift out over the sea, or a wave may develop along the equatorial trough (the band of low atmospheric pressure where the trade winds from both hemispheres converge). This will produce a depression that detaches itself and moves away from the equatorial trough, which reforms behind it. No matter what causes it, once it has formed the depression moves westward as an *easterly wave* (so called because it comes from the east).

Minor depressions can form anywhere, but one will grow into a hurricane only if it crosses a large expanse of very warm sea.

Figure 14: *Areas where hurricanes form and their direction of travel.*

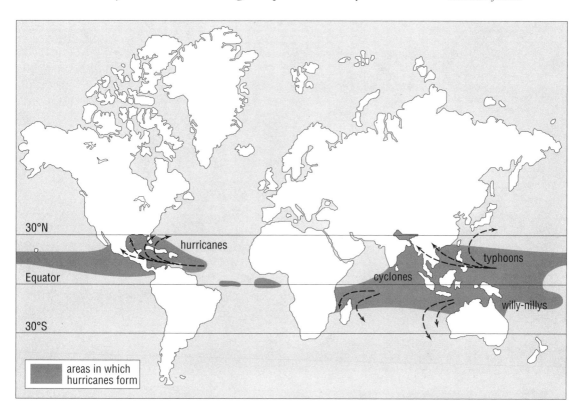

This confines the birthplace of hurricanes to the tropics. In latitudes higher than about 20° the sea-surface temperature is usually too low.

Close to the equator the sea is often warm enough to start a hurricane, but hurricanes never form in latitudes lower than 5°. The Coriolis effect is needed to swing the air moving toward the low-pressure area into a circular path. Precisely at the equator, there is no Coriolis effect (see box on page 40) and the effect is not strong enough to cause the necessary swing within 5° of the equator.

Vorticity (see page 38) will cause moving air to swing into a curved path and eventually start it rotating. After that the conservation of its angular momentum will accelerate the air as it converges into an ever smaller radius. Without assistance from the Coriolis effect, however, to generate winds of hurricane force at latitudes lower than 5°, air would need to converge on the low-pressure region from such a vast area that there is simply not enough air

Figure 15: *A GOES satellite photograph of Hurricane Allen taken on August 8, 1990.* (NOAA/NESDIS)

available. Even at 5°, air within a radius of more than 300 miles would need to contract to a radius of about 20 miles to produce winds of about 100 MPH. In contrast, at a latitude of 20°, air contracting from a radius of about 90 miles to 20 miles would produce 100-MPH winds. These areas are calculated without taking account of friction, which slows the rate at which wind speed increases. Allow for friction, and the areas must be increased.

Taken together, the need for a high sea-surface temperature and a sufficiently strong Coriolis effect confine the region in which tropical cyclones can form to a belt over the oceans between latitudes 5° and 20° in both hemispheres. They also restrict the time of year, because it is usually only in late summer and fall that the water is warm enough, although occasionally hurricanes develop outside these seasons.

Some tropical cyclones form in the east of the North Pacific, but the great majority do not develop until depressions have crossed to the western side of an ocean. This is also due, indirectly, to the Coriolis effect. Over the tropics, air moves vertically in Hadley cells (explained in box on page 20). As it moves away from the equator at a great height, the Coriolis effect causes the air to swing to the right in the northern hemisphere and to the left in the southern. In both hemispheres this is a swing to the east, and it makes the layer of high-level air moving away from the equator deeper on the eastern side of the Hadley cells than on the western side. This high-level air sinks while still over the tropics and warms adiabatically. This limits the upward movement of warm air rising from the surface by convection, because the rising air meets a layer of subsiding air that is warmer, and therefore less dense than itself and can rise no further. Sometimes the convection currents are vigorous enough to break through the inversion, but it is much easier for them to do so on the western than the eastern side of the Hadley cells where there is a thicker layer of sinking, warming air. This is why tropical cyclones develop on the western side of oceans.

Depressions can form over land or sea, in dry or moist air. To develop into a tropical cyclone, however, a depression must gather enough water vapor to provide a layer of very moist air deep enough to supply it with sufficient latent heat of condensation. This is why the depression must travel a long distance over a warm sea. If the depression moves over a continental land mass, it will not gain moisture and no tropical cyclone will develop. Many tropical depressions end in this way. Those that grow into hurricanes have already crossed an ocean; since tropical weather systems travel from east to west, that is another reason why most hurricanes begin on the western side of oceans.

There is one more difficulty. The equatorial trough rarely lies exactly at the equator. It moves north and south with the seasons and hurricanes develop only within about 60 miles of it. In the South

Atlantic the trough never moves south of 5°. This is too far north for the Coriolis effect to exert a strong enough influence on moving air, and so no hurricanes occur in the South Atlantic. Nor do they develop in the southeastern Pacific, because there the trough never moves south of the equator.

It is not only the equatorial trough that moves with the seasons. So does the jet stream. In winter it is quite far to the south, crossing northern Florida, but in summer it moves north. Figure 16 shows its approximate positions in January and July. In fact, there are two jet streams, the subtropical and the polar, but the subtropical is by far the more constant and so the term *jet stream* usually refers to the subtropical jet stream, which is the one shown in Figure 16.

Its position is important because a tropical cyclone cannot develop unless air is able to spiral upward unhindered. This requires that the wind speed and direction are more or less the same at all heights. Often they are not, a fact pilots use by studying the winds at different heights to decide the best altitude at which to fly. The spiraling air will be dissipated if it encounters a strong wind, and for this reason tropical cyclones cannot develop directly beneath the jet stream. It is very unlikely, therefore, that they can develop in winter over the Caribbean, because the jet stream is much too close (and it also blows more strongly in winter than in summer).

Figure 16: *Position of the jet stream in summer and winter.*

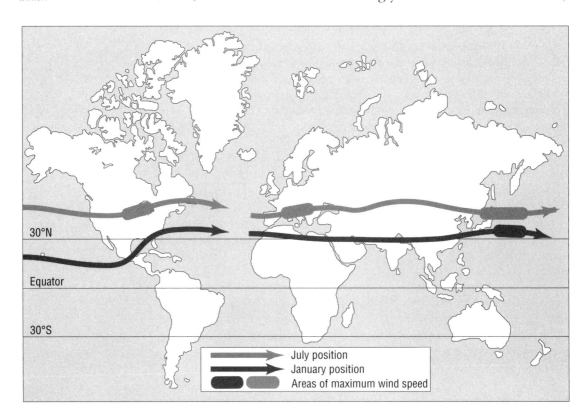

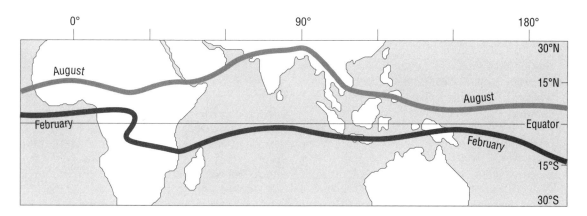

Figure 17: Seasonal movement of the equatorial trough.

In summer, however, any southward movement by the jet stream can encourage the development of tropical cyclones. It will never come so close as to interfere with their spiraling structure, but the edge of it may carry away air from the top of the cyclone, which will intensify it by drawing more air upward. By late summer and fall, the jet stream is starting to move south, so this is a favorable time for cyclones to grow.

The area in which hurricanes can be born is, therefore, confined to the western side of oceans, in latitudes lower than 20°, and between 5° and 10° of the equatorial trough (to its north in the northern hemisphere and to its south in the southern) when the trough itself is more than 5° away from the equator. Many begin to form in or close to the doldrums (see box on page 11), where the air is moving only slowly and they can grow undisturbed. They develop in late summer and fall, when the sea has warmed, and both the equatorial trough and the jet stream have started to move south.

Hurricane and storm tracks

Of all the tropical cyclones that occur each year, on average two-thirds are in the northern hemisphere and half of those begin in the western North Pacific. They are Asian typhoons. Hurricanes, affecting the Caribbean and western North Atlantic, account for only one-sixth of the northern-hemisphere total and only a little more than one-tenth of the world total. About one in ten of those in the northern hemisphere are cyclones, which develop in the northern Indian Ocean (those in the southern Indian Ocean are "typhoons").

Atlantic hurricanes and Asian typhoons are most likely to strike between July and October, baguios between September and

Global wind systems

Rising air produces low atmospheric pressure at the surface, into which air flows. Subsiding air produces high surface pressure, with air flowing outward. According to the three-cell model of atmospheric circulation, air rises at the equator, producing a region of low pressure into which trade winds blow from north and south. The winds converge at a low level, in the Intertropical Convergence Zone, a narrow belt to either side of the equator. In the tropics, therefore, the prevailing winds are the trades, from an easterly direction in both hemispheres.

Air descending in the low-latitude Hadley cells produces high pressure at around 30° in both hemispheres. Near the surface, the subsiding air diverges, some flowing back towards the equator and some flowing towards the poles. The air moving towards the poles is deflected by the Coriolis effect, to the right in the northern hemisphere and left in the southern. In both hemispheres this produces prevailing westerly winds.

There is a second region of low pressure at about 60° in both hemispheres. This is where the westerly winds flowing toward the poles encounter air spilling towards the equator from the high-pressure region over the poles, where air is subsiding and diverging. The two types of air meet at the polar front and rise. Air flowing away from the polar high-pressure regions is also deflected by the Coriolis effect. Deflection to the right in the northern hemisphere and to the left in the southern produces prevailing easterly winds.

Over the world as a whole, the prevailing surface winds form three belts in each hemisphere. They are easterly between 0° and 30°, westerly between 30° and 60°, and easterly between 60° and 90°.

At higher altitudes the prevailing winds in the tropics become westerly. The mid-latitude winds are westerly at all altitudes. High-level polar winds are westerly.

In mid-latitudes, these are the directions from which winds blow most commonly, but on any particular day they may blow from a different direction due to the passage of weather systems.

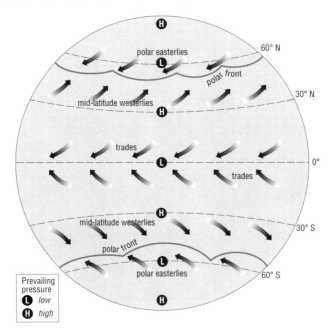

Global wind belts.

Figure 18: *Storm tracks across North America.*

November. In the southern hemisphere, typhoons in the Indian Ocean usually develop near Madagascar, and South Pacific typhoons, or willy-nillys, near Australia, between December and March. In summer, the equatorial trough moves north. Figure 17 shows its approximate positions in February and August. As it crosses the Bay of Bengal in May or June, cyclones develop close to it, and in September, as it moves south again, there is a second cyclone season.

Tropical cyclones develop in air that is moving westward. This reflects the trade-wind air movement in the tropics. Should they leave the tropics, they enter a region where the prevailing winds blow in the opposite direction from west to east and are affected by this movement.

Over the world as a whole, the total force of all the westerly winds is balanced by an equal force of easterly winds (see box on page 54). There is friction between moving air and the surface of land and sea. This slows the wind, but it also pulls at the surface of the Earth very slightly. If winds blowing from west to east were stronger than those blowing from east to west, over millions of years that drag would accelerate the rotation of the Earth, because it would

Weather fronts

During the First World War, the Norwegian meteorologist Vilhelm Bjerknes (see volume 6 for biographical details) discovered that air forms distinct masses. Because each mass differs in its average temperature, and therefore density, from adjacent masses, air masses do not mix readily. He called the boundary between two air masses a *front*.

Air masses move across the surface of land and sea, and so the fronts between them also move. Fronts are named according to the temperature of the air *behind* the front compared with that ahead of it. If the air behind the advancing front is warmer than the air ahead of it, it is a *warm front*. If the air behind the front is cooler, it is a *cold front*.

Frontal depression.
1) *Ana-front (air rising along both fronts*
2) *Kata-front (air sinking along both fronts)*

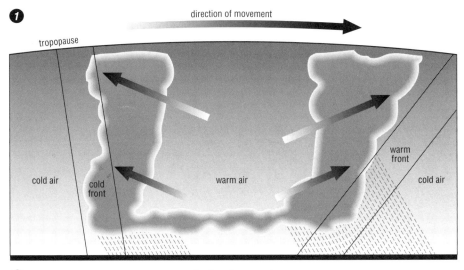

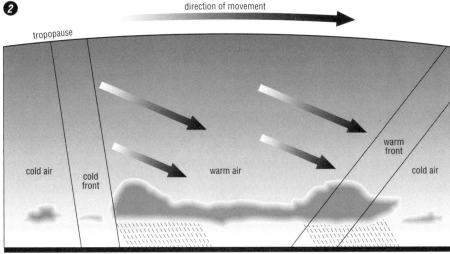

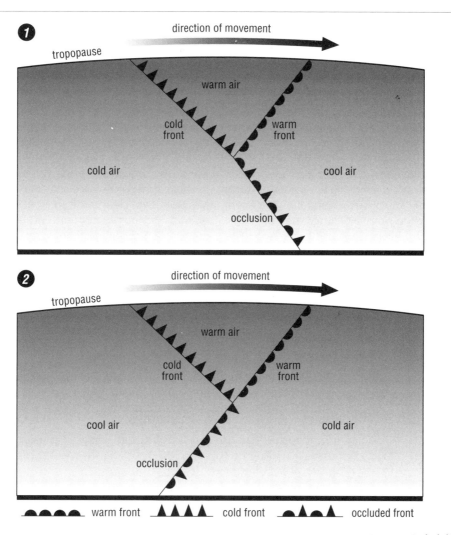

1

direction of movement

tropopause

warm air

cold
front

warm
front

cold air

cool air

occlusion

2

direction of movement

tropopause

warm air

cold
front

warm
front

cool air

cold air

occlusion

warm front   cold front   occluded front

Occluded fronts.

Fronts extend from the surface all the way to the tropopause, which is the boundary between the lower (troposphere) and upper (stratosphere) layers of the atmosphere. They slope upward, like the sides of a bowl, but the slope is very shallow. Warm fronts have a gradient of 1° or less, cold fronts of about 2°.

Cold fronts usually move faster across the surface of land and sea than warm fronts, so cold air tends to undercut warm air, raising it upward along the edge of the cold front. If warm air is rising, it will be raised even faster along the front separating it from cold air. The cold front is then called an *ana-front* and there is usually thick cloud and heavy rain or snow. If the warm air is sinking, because air at a low level is cooler than the air above it, an advancing cold front will raise it less. This is a *kata-front*, usually with only low-level cloud and light rain, drizzle, or fine snow. Both cold and warm fronts can be of the ana- or kata-front type; ana-fronts usually produce more cloud and precipitation than kata-fronts.

After a front has formed, advancing cold air pushes the warm air into what show on a weather map as a series of local bulges, and eventually distinct waves, where wedges of warm air lie between cold air. These are shown on weather maps and as they become steeper, areas of low pressure form at their crests. These are *frontal depressions*, which often bring wet weather. Just below what appears on weather maps as the wave crest, there is cold air to either side of a body of warm air. The cold front moves faster than the warm front, lifting the warm air along both fronts until all the warm air is clear of the surface. The fronts are then said to be *occluded*, and the pattern they form is called an *occlusion*.

Once the fronts are occluded and the warm air is no longer in contact with the surface, air to both sides of the occlusion is colder than the warm air. Occlusions can still be called cold or warm, however, because what matters is not the actual temperature of the air, but whether air to one side of a front or occlusion is warmer or cooler than the air behind it. In a cold occlusion the air ahead of the front is warmer than the air behind it and in a warm occlusion the air ahead is cooler, but both of these are cooler than the warm air that has been lifted clear of the surface. As the warm air is lifted, clouds usually form in it and often bring precipitation. Eventually the warm and cold air reach the same temperature, mix, and the frontal system dissipates.

amount to a force acting in the same direction. If the east-to-west winds were stronger, the Earth's rotation would be slowed.

Air pressure is generally low in the tropics, but around 30° from the equator lies the edge of a subtropical belt of mainly high pressure. Tropical cyclones form and travel not far from this region and many reach the edge of a local high-pressure system. They swing around the edge on a track that carries them away from the equator, traveling at 10 to 15 MPH, but as they enter higher latitudes sometimes accelerate to double that speed.

Most of those forming off the west coast of Central America follow tracks that take them into the middle of the Pacific, where they die without causing harm. Unfortunately, these are the exception. The great majority of tropical cyclones form on the western side of oceans, not far from continents, and move along tracks that carry them directly toward inhabited regions. Cyclones in the Indian Ocean swing north and head for the subcontinent, and Asian typhoons also swing north and head for Indonesia, China, and Japan. Atlantic hurricanes head for the islands of the Caribbean, then for the Gulf of Mexico or Florida and the United States mainland.

Although they start weakening as soon as they leave the warm, tropical ocean, tropical cyclones can travel a considerable distance over land while retaining enough energy to cause considerable damage. Their tracks continue to swing, however, and this may carry them back out to sea. Atlantic hurricanes occasionally cross the ocean and reach Europe.

Over the United States, hurricane tracks are similar to those of mid-latitude storms, shown in figure 18. These form over land or in coastal waters, and can be severe, with thunderstorms and winds of gale force. In places they can produce tornadoes. Tornadoes often form beneath the eyewalls of tropical cyclones, too, but there the similarity ends. Apart from being very much fiercer, tropical cyclones grow from slight disturbances in air that is otherwise at almost exactly the same temperature and pressure over a large area. Mid-latitude storms, on the other hand, form in association with weather fronts, the boundaries between masses of air at different temperatures and pressures (see box on page 56).

With the exception of the early summer cyclone season in the Bay of Bengal, tropical cyclones form in late summer and fall over the oceans throughout the tropics. They travel westward, then curve away from the equator. Those that survive long enough continue to follow curved tracks that eventually carry them in an easterly direction. Because almost all of them start life on the western side of oceans, a short westward journey is enough to take them over land and through inhabited areas. It is where they form and the direction in which they move that make them so dangerous.

Hurricanes in the United States and the Caribbean

At around 6 P.M. on the evening of October 5, 1995, screaming winds and torrential, lashing rains crossed the United States coast near Panama City, Florida, between Pensacola and Tallahassee. Opal, the second hurricane to assault the area in two months, was moving north from the Gulf of Mexico. Anticipating its arrival, the governors of Florida, Alabama, and Mississippi had declared states of emergency. People were compulsorily evacuated from coastal areas and offshore islands close to the hurricane's predicted path. All public buildings were closed in Pensacola and Mobile, Alabama. Staff controlling the emergency services moved into an underground bunker and the U.S. Navy removed all the aircraft from its Pensacola airbase.

By the time Opal reached Florida, its wind speed was falling. At its worst, when it was over the Yucatan Peninsula, in Mexico, the wind speed had risen to 150 MPH, with gusts stronger than that, but then they fell to below 130 MPH. Even so, it was ferocious enough. Five inches of rain fell during the night of October 5. That is considerably more than the 3.5 inches of rain Pensacola and Tallahassee ordinarily expect to receive in October.

Figure 19: *Track of Hurricane Hugo, September 1989.*

It was not so much the wind or rain people feared, however, but the sea. The hurricane brought huge breakers, and as the wind drove water toward the coast the sea rose 12 feet above its usual high-tide level. Homes near beaches were washed away and small boats were plucked from their moorings and hurled ashore. The storm-driven sea and wind killed 13 people in the United States, having already killed 50 in Mexico and Guatemala. The damage it caused in Florida and Alabama was estimated to have cost about $4 billion.

Opal continued to move north at about 25 MPH, but weakening all the time. Some nine hours after it crossed the Florida coast it was about 55 miles east of Huntsville, Alabama, and had been reclassified as a tropical storm, although it was still bringing heavy rain and gale-force winds.

This hurricane was the 15th of the 1995 season and the ninth to strike the Gulf Coast. Several storms faded harmlessly far from land, but had Opal not weakened so quickly it might well have proved one of the most violent of the century. In other respects it was fairly typical.

It formed over Yucatan on September 27, and by the end of the month had intensified sufficiently to be classed as a tropical storm. It continued to grow fiercer and on October 2 it was reclassified as a hurricane. Four days later it was already dying. Four days is the average life expectancy for an Atlantic hurricane.

During its brief life, Opal moved almost directly north. Had it lasted longer, by then reduced to a tropical storm rather than being a full hurricane, its track would have probably curved to the east, much like Hurricane Hugo, which crossed the United States and Canada in 1989. Hugo lasted much longer and followed a more complete track, as shown in figure 19.

Hugo began to form on September 11 in the eastern North Atlantic, not far from the African coast (the numbers on the map are the dates in September and the location of the storm on those dates). By the next day it had become a tropical depression. It was a tropical storm by the 14th and a hurricane by the 19th. Typically, its track had carried it westward and as it developed into a hurricane it swung northwest, crossing the coast at Charleston, South Carolina, at about 10 P.M. on the night of the 21st. Moving at an average speed of 29 MPH, by the 23rd its track was curving towards the east and on that day and the next it crossed the northeastern United States. Its passage over land had isolated it from the warm water needed to sustain it, so by the time it reached North Carolina it had weakened to a tropical storm. It moved through Québec and Labrador, Canada, on the 24th and on the 25th it crossed the coast again, moving out into the North Atlantic and heading northeast, now as an extratropical storm.

Throughout its journey across eastern North America, the eye of Hugo had a diameter of 30 miles, which is large. Some are no more than five miles across. A large eye means the entire storm is large, because the hurricane forms as circles around the eye. Hugo covered a vast area within which it caused a great deal of damage, estimated to have cost about $10.5 billion in the United States. This made it possibly the most destructive hurricane in American history in financial terms, though fortunately few lives were lost.

Figure 20: *West Palm Beach, September 1947. Broken palm trees attest to the violent winds of a recent hurricane.*
(American Red Cross)

Hurricanes develop quickly, but nowadays satellite monitoring gives the U.S. authorities several days to prepare for their arrival. As Hugo approached, about 12,000 people in Charleston were evacuated into shelters, although some who sought safety in Charlotte, North Carolina, found they had placed themselves directly in the hurricane's path. There were only four deaths in the continental United States: one in Charleston, one in Charlotte, and two in Virginia. In fact, Charleston was lucky. The eye of Hugo passed to the east, exposing the city to the less violent winds on the left side of the storm (where the winds blow in the opposite direction to that in which the hurricane is traveling, reducing their speed). Had the eye crossed the coast just 20 miles further south, Charleston would have experienced the full force of the much more dangerous right side of the storm (where the 29 MPH at which the storm was moving would have added to the speed of the spiraling wind).

The Caribbean islands fared worse. They are more exposed and have less time to prepare because the storm is already close to them when it first develops. Hugo reached first Guadeloupe and then Dominica, in the Leeward Islands, on September 17, and the U.S.

Virgin Islands and Puerto Rico on the 19th. There was time in Puerto Rico to warn shipping to clear the area, close the airport, and organize street patrols to prevent the looting that took place in the wake of the storm in St. Thomas and St. Croix, in the Virgin Islands, but the death toll was high. Eleven people were killed in Guadeloupe, 10 in Montserrat, six in the Virgin Islands, and 12 in Puerto Rico.

Atlantic hurricanes travel west, then north, and finally east, but not all of them reach the United States. In 1988, for example, 11 tropical storms developed in the Atlantic, including five hurricanes; three of these storms generated winds of more than 131 MPH, but only four of them crossed the United States coast and one of the hurricanes, Gilbert, came close enough for its outer margins to cause some damage in Texas. If a hurricane develops far enough to the east, its curving track may carry it parallel to the coast of Florida and the Carolinas, over the ocean, and communities on land will escape its full force, partly because they are well clear of the eye and partly because at all times they are to the left of the eye, in the quarter where the wind speed is lower.

That is how the United States escaped Luis, the 12th hurricane of the 1995 season, which struck the U.S. Virgin Islands and Puerto Rico on September 6. With an eye 60 miles across and a total diameter of about 700 miles, covering a total surface area of about 385,000 square miles, Luis was even bigger than Hugo in 1989, although with winds gusting up to 140 MPH it was not quite so fierce. Traveling west at about 12 MPH, it struck Guadeloupe, the U.S. Virgin Islands, and Puerto Rico. As is usually the case, the sea did as much damage as the wind and torrential rain, rising up to nine feet above its usual high-tide level. In Guadeloupe, a huge wave swept a French tourist to his death as he was trying to photograph the sea. The Caribbean islands are popular tourist destinations and airlines, tour operators, and foreign governments all issue warnings to their customers or citizens. In this case, Thomas Cook, a British tour operator, flew its customers to Barbados or Miami, and the British Foreign Office advised travelers to avoid the area or, if they were there already, to remain in secure accommodations and follow the instructions of the local authorities.

Puerto Rico, the U.S. Virgin Islands, and the countries of Central America suffer more from hurricanes than most countries. In September, 1995, for example, Hurricane Marilyn destroyed four-fifths of the houses on St. Thomas in the Virgin Islands, although the only casualties occurred among people on boats when the storm struck. Of those, three died and 100 were injured or missing. The team arriving by air with emergency supplies said none of the buildings on St. Thomas appeared to have roofs. Hurricane Roxanne, which brought 115-MPH winds to Mexico in

Figure 21: *1960 damage from Hurricane Donna in Islamadoro, Florida.* (American Red Cross)

October, 1995, killed at least 14 people and tens of thousands were forced to leave their homes.

From September 12 to 17, 1988, Gilbert, one of the worst of all hurricanes in recent years, ravaged Jamaica and Mexico, killing at least 260 people. Then it moved into Texas, where it triggered nearly 40 tornadoes and caused property damage costing an estimated $10 billion, although by that time its force had largely abated and farmers in Texas welcomed the rain it brought.

A minor deflection in the trade winds comprising the easterly wave that would develop into Gilbert was first noticed on September 3 as a group of clouds moving westwards over the ocean, away from the coast of West Africa. It was designated a tropical storm on September 9, when its wind speeds exceeded 39 MPH. That was the day it moved through the Lesser Antilles. A day later, with wind speeds exceeding 74 MPH, it officially became a hurricane and within about 12 hours its winds had increased to more than 96 MPH. On the 11th the National Hurricane Center in the United States warned the Jamaican authorities to expect a hurricane with winds in excess of 100 MPH in the next 12 to 24 hours. When it reached Jamaica, passing over Kingston around noon on September 12, the winds were more than 111 MPH and the hurricane was still intensifying. When its center passed about 20 miles to the south of Grand Cayman Islands, at 9 A.M. on September 13, its winds (on the dangerous northern side) were blowing at more than 131 MPH and two hours later they exceeded 155 MPH. By 6 P.M. on September 13 the atmospheric pressure in the eye was 888 mb, the lowest ever recorded for an Atlantic hurricane. The storm reached the Mexican coast on September 14. A Cuban ship several miles out at sea was thrown onto the shore as the sea rose by 20 feet. Its eyewall began weakening as the hurricane moved inland, but away from the center the winds retained their force for some time longer. Once the eyewall disappeared, however, it did not form again.

When a hurricane does reach the United States coast, adequate early warning and efficient, experienced emergency services minimize casualties. Property is not so easily protected, however, and over the years as hurricanes have killed and injured ever fewer people, the cost of hurricane damage has increased. This is because vulnerable areas are very popular as places to live. Hurricanes are likely to cross the coast of the United States anywhere along a stretch of about 2,000 miles from Texas, on the Gulf of Mexico, around Florida, and to Virginia on the Atlantic. The number of people living along this coastline has roughly doubled since the 1930s and there are now more people living in the Miami and Fort Lauderdale area of Florida than lived along the entire 2,000 miles earlier in this century. To make matters worse, many of them live in mobile homes. Not only can a hurricane demolish such dwellings entirely, but in doing so it can hurl debris from them against other buildings to cause further damage. According to Lloyds of London, the biggest insurance organization in the world, between 1966 and 1987 there was no single natural disaster costing more than $1 billion in insurance claims, but between 1987 and 1992 there were 10 wind storms with a combined cost of more than $15 billion.

Camille, a hurricane that struck Missouri and Louisiana in 1969, illustrates this. Of comparable strength to Gilbert, in 1988, but with a higher eye pressure (905 mb), it killed some 250 people living along the coast and 125 more died in the flooding it caused. The cost of the damage it did to property came to $1.42 billion. In 1989, however, Hugo caused 43 deaths and damage in the U.S. costing $10.5 billion and in 1995 Opal caused 13 U.S. (and 50 Central American) deaths and property damage costing $4 billion.

Hurricane Camille illustrates the further point that hurricanes may interact with other weather systems. Camille was very strong, but it had weakened to a tropical storm when it turned east and crossed the Blue Ridge Mountains in Virginia. There its winds gathered moist air moving inland from the Atlantic and funneled it through the two narrow valleys of the Rockfish and Tye Rivers. Then this moist air met an advancing cold front that was already producing thunderstorms. The moist, low-pressure air rose up the front (see box 15 on page 56) and produced 18 inches of rain in a matter of hours. Most of the damage Camille caused was due to the resulting floods.

There were at least 17 Atlantic hurricanes in 1995, more than double the number in 1994. When tropical storms that failed to develop into full hurricanes are included, the 1995 season was more active than any for more than 60 years. Ordinarily in recent years there have been an average of nine or 10 named storms and six hurricanes. It may be, however, that what appears now to have been a bad year may turn out to be fairly typical over a longer period.

Some scientists believe there have been unusually few Atlantic hurricanes in the last 25 years. They suggest atmospheric conditions over Africa and the tropical Pacific are now returning to the patterns they used to have many years ago and that these patterns tend to generate more easterly waves in the Atlantic than those of recent years (see page 33). If they are correct, hurricanes may be more frequent in years to come.

Hurricanes that reach Europe

As hurricanes go, Charley was nothing special. It reached the coast of North Carolina on August 17, 1986, moved north along the coast of Maryland, then turned east and headed out over the Atlantic. It caused little damage. Indeed, it brought welcome rain to farmers in the Carolinas, Virginia, and Maryland. There were only three Atlantic hurricanes in that year and none was particularly strong.

Charley, the gentle hurricane, might have been forgotten, only it persisted. Its track carried it right across the North Atlantic and a few days later it reached Britain. By this time it was classified as only a storm. Its warm eyewall had cooled and its winds weakened. Nevertheless, in southwest Wales people were unprepared for its arrival and it caused a great deal of damage. Although officially it was no longer a hurricane, it retained the essential structure of one. It still had the remains of an eyewall of cloud, bringing torrential rain, and behind that the eye, in which the sky was clear and the air still. The eye was followed by the second side of the eyewall, and even fiercer winds. It took two days and the night between to pass. The combination of rain and high seas caused widespread flooding. An inshore lifeboat had to rescue vacationers from one inland trailer park. Dyfed, the northern part of which took the full force of the storm, is the county occupying the peninsula of southwest Wales. It is mainly rural, a sparsely populated place of farms, hills, and small villages. This limited the damage to property. The next hurricane to strike Britain did so in England, with much worse consequences.

Hurricanes can retain their strength as they cross the Atlantic, arriving with enough power to wreak considerable havoc. Floyd, the last hurricane of the 1987 season, formed on October 9, and on the 12th its winds reached more than 75 MPH, the lowest speed to qualify it as a hurricane. It passed through the Florida Keys, but had weakened to less than hurricane force within 12 hours. Then it headed out over the ocean.

European meteorologists saw it coming, but miscalculated its track. This is easily done, because a degree or two can make a great deal of difference. The meteorologists believed that Floyd would pass through the English Channel, well south of the British coast, then head into the North Sea, weakening all the time. Obviously, it would endanger shipping, and the English Channel is one of the busiest sea lanes in the world, but they said people on shore had nothing to fear. It arrived on the night of October 15, traveling a few degrees to the left of its predicted path, and caused havoc throughout the densely populated towns and villages of southern England. Though barely a hurricane in the strict sense, its winds gusted to more than 80 MPH and by dawn on the 16th, 19 million trees had been uprooted. The storm killed 19 people and the damage cost about $2.25 billion (£1.5 billion).

For Scots everywhere, the evening of January 25 is Burns Night, when haggis is paraded to the sound of the bagpipes, a certain amount of whisky is drunk, and the poet is honored by reading aloud from his works. On that day in 1990, Britain, along with much of northwest Europe, suffered the fiercest storm for many years. This time, although it was technically a storm rather than a hurricane, winds reached more than 100 MPH. Its track was predicted accurately, but there was nothing anyone could do to protect property. Roofs were torn from buildings, trees uprooted, power lines brought down, and transport and communications seriously disrupted. Most of Britain was affected and about 47 people died. The storm then moved into continental Europe, killing 19 people in The Netherlands, 10 in Belgium, eight in France, seven in Germany, and four in Denmark. Soon after that, on February 3, 29 people died when winds of hurricane force struck France and Germany, and then on February 26, another wind storm killed at least 51 people in Britain, The Netherlands, Germany, France, Belgium, Switzerland, Ireland, and Italy.

Winds strong enough to qualify a storm as a hurricane occur in Europe every few years. In December 1993, for example, a windstorm killed 12 people in Britain, and on January 25 and 26, 1989, hurricane-force winds killed at least 12 people in Spain.

Air masses and the weather they bring

As air moves slowly across the surface it is sometimes warmed, sometimes cooled; in some places water evaporates into it, and in others it loses moisture. Its characteristics change.

When it crosses a very large region, such as a continent or ocean, its principal characteristics are evened out and over a vast area all the air is at much the same temperature and pressure and is equally moist or dry. Such a body of air is called an *air mass*.

Air masses are warm, cool, moist, or dry according to the region over which they formed and are named accordingly. The names and their abbreviations are straightforward. Continental (c) air masses form over continents, maritime (m) ones over oceans. Depending on the latitude in which they form, air masses may be Arctic (A), polar (P), tropical (T), or equatorial (E). Except in the case of equatorial air, these categories are then combined to give continental Arctic (cA), maritime Arctic (mA), continental po-

lar (cP), maritime polar (mP), continental tropical (cT), and maritime tropical (mT).

North America is affected by mP, cP, cT, and mT air, the maritime air masses originating over the Pacific, Atlantic, or Gulf. As they move from where they formed (called their *source regions*) air masses change, but they do so slowly and at first they bring with them the weather conditions that produced them. As their names suggest, maritime air is moist, continental air is dry, polar air is cool, and tropical air is warm. At the surface there is little difference between polar and Arctic air, but above about 15,000 feet, Arctic air is colder.

It is cP air spilling south when the cT and mT move towards the equator in the fall that brings cold, dry winters to the central United States. It is the meeting of mT air from the Gulf and cT air from inland that produces fierce storms in the southeast of the country.

The mid-1980s was a time of little hurricane activity. The Atlantic was quiet. Few tropical storms developed, few of those grew into hurricanes, and those that did were generally weak. Weak storms are just as likely to cross the ocean as strong ones, however, because what matters is not the size or power of the storm, but the distance it travels over land. Over the ocean, hurricanes are sustained by a limitless supply of water. It is evaporating sea water and spray that releases latent heat to feed the vigorous convection needed to build the warm, towering clouds of the eyewall. If, like Charley and Floyd, a hurricane turns north without penetrating the American mainland, there is a chance it will turn east before it begins to weaken significantly.

When steady wind speeds exceed 75 MPH, they are rated as hurricane force on the Beaufort scale (see box on page 46), but in Europe they are not really hurricanes, even if that is how they began, far away in the tropical Atlantic. They lack the extreme violence of a tropical cyclone because they are not fed by a very warm sea, and most European "hurricanes" are associated with frontal systems. Tropical cyclones are not frontal.

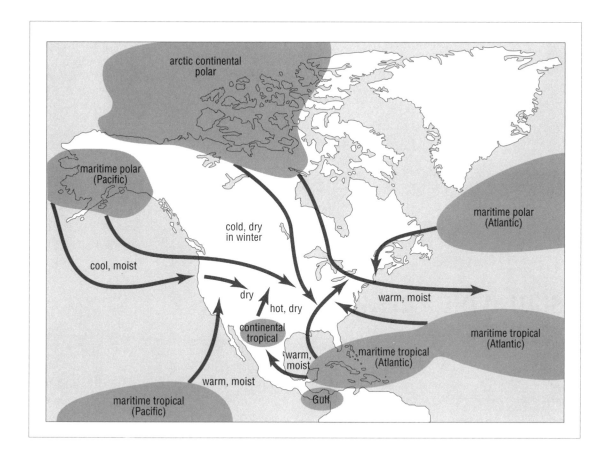

arctic continental polar

maritime polar (Pacific)

maritime polar (Atlantic)

cold, dry in winter

cool, moist

dry

hot, dry

warm, moist

continental tropical

maritime tropical (Atlantic)

warm, moist

maritime tropical (Atlantic)

warm, moist

Gulf

maritime tropical (Pacific)

Over the tropics, the air temperature and pressure is fairly constant throughout vast areas and a very small disturbance is enough to trigger the development of a tropical cyclone. In mid-latitudes the situation is very different. Air masses with very different characteristics cross constantly, mainly from west to east (see box), and where two air masses meet while moving at different speeds, a front develops (see box on page 56). Where a warm and cold front meet at surface level, there is often a region of low pressure called a *depression*. Air flowing toward a depression is deflected by the Coriolis effect into a spiraling path around it, and the greater the difference in pressure between the center of the depression and the air surrounding it, the stronger the winds will be. As they approach the center, the conservation of their angular momentum causes the winds to increase in speed.

Mid-latitude depressions can be deep, and therefore the winds around them can be strong. Winds often reach gale force and at sea they can reach hurricane force of more than 75 MPH. Winds of this strength are uncommon over land because their passage over

Air masses affecting North America.

uneven ground generates friction, which slows them, but now and then one crosses a coast and may even penetrate deep inland.

To a meteorologist, tropical and mid-latitude depressions are cyclones, regions of low pressure around which air flows *cyclonically* (counterclockwise in the northern hemisphere), and any cyclone can produce strong winds. Although a tropical cyclone forms in the absence of fronts and most mid-latitude cyclones are frontal, the principal difference is found at the center. A tropical cyclone forms over very warm water and turns into a hurricane when it develops an eye and eyewall at a markedly higher temperature than the surrounding air. A mid-latitude cyclone lacks this warm core. It is the warmth that drives the hurricane, and without it mid-latitude depressions may produce fierce storms, but they can never grow into full-scale hurricanes.

Asian typhoons and cyclones

On November 2, 1995, winds of 140 MPH swept the eastern Philippines. This was Angela, the first typhoon of the 1995 season, and by the time it passed at least 35 people had died and 50 were missing. The typhoon destroyed 15,000 homes and more than 200,000 people were left homeless.

In Mandarin Chinese, *ta feng* means *big wind* and in some Chinese dialects it is pronounced *tai fung*. It is the name people give to the ferocious tropical cyclones that form in the South China Sea. These can devastate offshore islands and often cross the mainland coast, sometimes traveling a considerable distance inland and leaving a trail of destruction and human misery. Borrowing the Chinese phrase, we call these cyclones *typhoons* and extend the name to all tropical cyclones forming over the Pacific.

The name is not used consistently, however. The term *baguio* is sometimes used to identify tropical cyclones occurring near Indonesia and *willy-nilly* or *cyclone* for those near Australia. Cyclone, in the sense of a tropical cyclone rather than the strict meteorological sense of a low-pressure region around which air moves cyclonically (counterclockwise in the northern hemisphere), was once the name reserved for those occurring in the northern Indian Ocean, although nowadays tropical cyclones occurring in the southern Indian Ocean are often called cyclones as well.

Of all the tropical cyclones that form, almost 90% are typhoons or cyclones. Eastern Asia, the Indian subcontinent, Indonesia, the Philippines, and the smaller islands of the tropical Pacific suffer nine such visitations for every one that occurs in the Atlantic and Caribbean, and Pacific typhoons are often fiercer than Atlantic hurricanes. This is probably due to the fact that the Pacific is much wider than the Atlantic. Developing storms have much farther to travel before reaching a continent and losing their source of water, and so they have more time in which to grow and intensify. For the same reason, a typhoon can cover a much larger area than a hurricane. "Supertyphoons" are rare, but when they occur they can cover three million square miles, an area equal to that of the mainland United States.

Angela was a typical typhoon, not least in striking the Philippines, which endure several in most years. Even those tropical storms that fail to grow into full-scale typhoons can cause considerable harm. Tropical Storm Zack, for example, caused serious flooding in the Philippines in October 1995, and killed nearly 60 people by capsizing a ship sailing between two of the islands.

It is the wind we associate most closely with typhoons. Winds of more than 75 MPH (hurricane force) may extend around the eye to a diameter of 300 miles, so they affect an area of more than 70,000 square miles, but winds of gale force (more than 40 MPH) can also cause considerable damage in the area surrounding the fiercest winds. In a tropical cyclone 300 miles in diameter, there are gales up to 240 miles from the center. This adds more than 110,000 square miles to the total area affected.

Figure 22: *While operating in the South China Sea, USNS* Spica *battles 14-foot seas and 40 knots of wind to provide supplies for the* USS *Kitty Hawk. The heavy seas and wind were caused by Typhoon Orchid, September 29, 1994.* (U.S. Navy)

Monsoon

Our word *monsoon* comes originally from an Arabic word, *mawsim*, which means *season*. Monsoons are strongly marked seasons. In Asia the winter monsoon is dry and the summer monsoon brings heavy rain.

Monsoons resemble land and sea breezes, but occur on a huge scale. They are due to the different rates at which the land and sea warm and cool. During summer, the land heats much faster than the sea. Warm air rises over the land, forming a large area in which the atmospheric pressure is lower than it is over the cooler sea. This draws in air that is moist from its contact with the ocean surface. In winter, the reverse happens. The land cools rapidly and pressure rises over it. Air flows from land to sea and, because the air originates deep inside a continent, it is very dry. So there is a dry winter monsoon and a warm wet summer monsoon.

Monsoon climates occur over most of the tropics. They affect much of tropical Africa, the northern part of Madagascar, the southern part of the Arabian peninsula, the Indian subcontinent, southern Asia, eastern Asia as far north as Japan, and northern Australia. Parts of North America also have a monsoon climate. West of the Rockies it brings a dry summer and rainy winter. On the eastern side of the continent the summer is wet and the winter dry. Monsoons are strongest over southern Asia, however, because of other seasonal changes in the distribution of air masses.

During the summer, the equatorial trough moves north, intensifying the low pressure over land. At the same time, the Himalaya Mountains are so high they divide the air circulating over Asia into two distinct masses. In winter, the jet stream lies over the mountains and the polar high-pressure area covers most of northern Asia. Air flowing outward from it intensifies the offshore winds. In summer, the jet stream weakens as the continent warms, reducing the difference in air temperature to the north and south of the mountains.

Wind is only one of the hazards, however. Torrential rain is at least as dangerous and it is not unusual for a tropical cyclone to deliver 20 inches of rain in the space of 48 hours. The record is held by a typhoon that brought more than 64 inches of rain to the Philippines in just a few hours. Rainfall in the Philippines is heaviest in summer, between July and October. In the north this is due to the influence of the Asian monsoon (see box above), but in the south it is due mainly to typhoons. Even so, the wettest places expect no more than 20 inches of rain in the rainiest month, so the typhoon delivered more than three times what is usually the heaviest monthly rainfall.

Tropical cyclones in the Pacific and Indian Oceans are often severe. Geralda, a typhoon (or cyclone) that struck Madagascar from February 2 to 4, 1994, brought torrential rains driven by winds of up to 220 MPH. It left at least 70 people dead and half a million homeless, almost totally destroyed the country's principal port, and flooded more than two-thirds of its farmland. Geralda was described as the "cyclone of the century," but there have been others almost as fierce. On May 2, 1994, a cyclone with winds of up to 180 MPH moving north across the Bay of Bengal crossed islands at the mouth of the Ganges, in Bangladesh. It killed more than 200 people. The death toll would have been even higher but for an early warning system that gave time for a major evacuation. A cyclone that reached the coastal islands of Bangladesh on April 30, 1991, before the early warning system was established, killed at least 131,000 people. In an average year about six cyclones form in the Bay of Bengal.

Like all tropical cyclones, those of the eastern hemisphere form between latitudes 5° and 20°, but unlike the Atlantic, where no tropical cyclones form south of the equator, in the Pacific they develop in both northern and southern hemispheres. They travel west, in both hemispheres, then follow tracks carrying them away from the equator, heading north in the northern hemisphere and south in the southern. In the southern hemisphere, of course, the Coriolis effect makes their winds spiral clockwise around the eye.

Except for those few that develop off the east coast of Central America and usually move out to sea, Pacific storm tracks carry them toward densely populated lands. Cyclones cross the coasts of India, Pakistan, and Bangladesh, and some, moving north through the Arabian Sea, reach Oman. South of the equator, they move towards Madagascar, some passing to the west of the island into the Mozambique Channel between Madagascar and Mozambique. In March 1994 a typhoon left 1.5 million people homeless in Mozambique.

The Ganges, India's greatest river, flows sluggishly and its level varies greatly. During the dry winter it carries little water and the level is low, but in spring it rises as meltwater from the Himalayas pours into it. It reaches its highest levels during the heavy monsoon rains of summer. This is also the time of year when cyclones are most likely to form to the south, in the Bay of Bengal, and move north. Although the Asian monsoon is strongest in India, it also affects all of southern Asia, and on a smaller scale there is also a monsoon season in tropical Africa.

Most of Bangladesh is low-lying, with fertile plains nourished by silt deposited when the rivers flood. It is in Bangladesh that the Ganges, known as the Padma at this point, joins India's other great river, the Brahmaputra, known locally as the Jamuna, and the combined rivers, known as the Meghna, flow towards the sea, swelled further by the many smaller tributaries which join them. Where the river enters the sea it forms a large delta. The Meghna has no single "mouth," but many mouths, the individual branches of the river weaving their tortuous courses through a maze of islands and, in the south, an almost completely uninhabited region of mangrove swamp called the Sundarbans. The northern delta is inhabited by people whose homes are built on earth platforms or embankments to keep them clear of the seasonal floods when all the river channels merge into a single stream.

Figure 23: *The USS* Hornet, *showing 25 feet of collapsed deck from a typhoon in June 1945.* (U.S. Navy)

Bangladesh is one of the most densely populated countries in the world, with an average of nearly 2,000 people to every square mile, and most of them live in the countryside. Fish and other aquatic animals such as prawns are their most important source of dietary protein. Most are freshwater species, caught by fishermen who live in the countless villages beside rivers and in the northern part of the delta. When a cyclone strikes, they have little protection. After tropical storms on April 17, 1994, 200 fishermen from the town of Cox's Bazar were missing and feared drowned; 5,000 fishermen were missing from coastal islands after a cyclone in 1991, which caused at least 131,000 deaths. Even this was not the most severe storm recorded. A cyclone in November 1970 left some 500,000 Bangladeshi people dead. It was one of the worst natural disasters of this century.

As typhoons move westward across the Pacific, their tracks are likely to bring them close to many small islands and then to the Malay Archipelago, the largest in the world. Indonesia, occupying the larger part of the archipelago and with an area of about 741,000 square miles, is a string of about 3,000 islands straddling the equator and stretching more than 3,000 miles from the Malay Peninsula to New Guinea. Geographically, the Indonesian islands are joined to the Philippines. These cover a smaller area, of about

116,000 square miles, but comprise 1,000 inhabited islands and 6,107 uninhabited ones.

Most of Indonesia lies to the west of the usual typhoon tracks, which are turning north by the time they reach the islands, although Indonesia does not escape entirely. Turning north, however, the storms head directly for the islands lying between Indonesia and China, the Philippines.

Much of the northern coast of Australia north of about 20° S is exposed to Pacific typhoons, although severe ones are rare so far south. On Christmas Day in 1974, however, the country experienced its worst natural disaster ever when Cyclone Tracy devastated the northern city of Darwin. The cyclone started to form on December 21 over the Arafura Sea between Australia and New Guinea. In the following days it intensified and moved southwestward on a track carrying it towards the Timor Sea, south of Timor, and from there it was expected to move into the Indian Ocean. Forecasters predicted it would remain at least 60 miles from the Australian coast. Then, on Christmas Eve, Tracy intensified still further and changed course, now heading southeast and directly towards Australia. It reached Darwin at 4 A.M., with winds of up to 150 MPH. The storm lashed the city for about four hours. By the time it moved away more than 50 people had lost their lives, 48,000 had been evacuated, and 90% of the buildings had been destroyed, including 8,000 homes.

Perhaps the most vulnerable regions of all are south and east Asia. By the time they reach eastern Indonesia, many typhoons are turning north toward the Philippines, Vietnam, China, and, beyond them, Korea and Japan. Ten people died in August 1994 in Taiwan in a fairly weak typhoon, with 85-MPH winds, but typhoons in that part of the East China Sea can be much worse. On August 20 and 21 of the same year, Typhoon Fred battered Zhejiang Province, China, for 43 hours without a break. It killed about 1,000 people and caused damage costing an estimated $1.1 billion. The same region suffered twice in August 1990, when Typhoon Yancy killed 216 people in Fujian and Zhejiang Provinces and Typhoon Abe killed 48 people in Zhejiang. The following year Typhoon Amy killed at least 35 people in southern China. It is appropriate that we derive our name for such storms from the Chinese.

Taiwan lies at the southern end of the East China Sea, where tropical cyclones formed in the South China Sea are turning north. Still further north lie the islands of Japan. Japan, in the East China Sea but between about 30° N and 45° N, might be thought safe from all but occasional typhoons that have weakened to tropical storms by the time they arrive, but typhoons often retain their power long enough for them to travel considerable distances.

In 1953 about one-third of the Japanese city of Nagoya, just north of latitude 35° N on the island of Honshu, was destroyed by a typhoon that left one million people homeless. This was far from the most devastating tropical cyclone the Japanese have had to endure. Hokkaido, the northernmost island, was struck by a tropical storm in 1954 that left 1,600 people dead, and in September 1959 Honshu suffered the worst typhoon in modern Japanese history. Called Vera, it killed more than 4,000 people and left 1.5 million homeless.

About once a year, two typhoons approach within about 900 miles of each other. This is close enough for them to interact and they start to turn around their common center, much like two stars orbiting their common center of gravity that lies somewhere between them. If the typhoons are of approximately equal size, they will turn around a point more or less halfway between their two centers. If one is much larger than the other, they will turn about a point closer to the larger one. This is called the Fujiwara effect. It was first described in 1921 by the Japanese meteorologist Sakuhei Fujiwara.

Arctic and Antarctic hurricanes

Resolution is a research ship designed to study the ocean floor. Its work forms part of the Ocean Drilling Program, an international scientific project that involves examining rock and sediment collected as cores drilled from the seabed. Its drilling rig, the pipes carried on its deck, and the hole through its hull down which the drillpipes pass make it a little unwieldy, but *Resolution* is big and tough. Built in 1985, it measures 470 feet from stem to stern and it is meant to survive anything the sea can throw at it. In the fall of 1995 *Resolution* came close to sinking in an Atlantic storm.

The voyage began uneventfully. *Resolution* set sail from Iceland in late September with 120 people on board, heading for the Greenland Sea, deep inside the Arctic Circle to the east of Greenland. The weather was not good, but *Resolution* sailed unperturbed through conditions that would have caused difficulties for a smaller vessel. Edwin G. Oonk, the captain, had to maneuver the ship repeatedly to avoid icebergs drifting out from the glaciers of Greenland, to the west.

Then the air pressure began falling sharply. There was a severe storm to the east, another to the south, and icebergs between *Resolution* and the Greenland coast, where the ship might have sheltered. Captain Oonk decided to sail forward into the weather. His tactic might have worked, but the two storms merged, pressure dropped still further, and the wind speed increased.

For two days the storm raged. The dial on the windspeed indicator had a maximum reading of 115 MPH and that was what it read in the gusts. Meeting waves 70 feet high, like solid walls of water, the ship rose high into the air and plunged into the troughs. At times the main propellers were lifted clear of the water. Lookouts, securely lashed down, had to be stationed in the stern to watch for icebergs, because at times the ship was being carried backwards at more than 4 MPH. After a day and a half of this, *Resolution* was in danger of sinking. The storm abated at last, and the vessel made its slow way to port for repairs.

This was not a tropical cyclone, but it was as fierce as one. Its winds of more than 115 MPH were classified as storm force 12+ (12 is hurricane force on the Beaufort scale of wind strength). In lower latitudes it would have been rated a category 3 hurricane, strong enough to uproot large trees and wreck mobile homes. In 1954, the Swedish meteorologist Tor Bergeron called storms of this force *extratropical hurricanes.*

They are very similar in some ways to tropical cyclones and occur in both north and south polar regions. Around Cape Horn, at the southernmost tip of South America, the frequent gales led sailors to name the latitudes the "roaring forties," "furious fifties," and "shrieking sixties." This region of frequent gales extends all the way around the world and is not confined to the area south of Cape Horn. It is associated with Cape Horn only because South America projects into the belt and before the Panama Canal was built ships were compelled to pass through it in order to cross between the Atlantic and Pacific. At Byrd Station, Antarctica, the wind is strong enough to produce severe gales about two-thirds of the time.

Occasionally the weather systems that cause them can bring severe weather to places in lower latitudes. Around Christmas, 1995, for example, one extended south and brought extreme cold and heavy snow to Scotland and northern England, with snowdrifts 30 feet deep in the Shetlands, the northernmost group of Scottish islands. It reduced December temperatures over Britain to 4° F below the monthly average and prevented 1995 from being the warmest year on record, although it was still the third warmest since 1659.

Extratropical hurricanes usually develop from *polar lows.* These are areas of relatively low atmospheric pressure that form near the edge of the sea ice. There, the air temperature over the ice can fall locally as low as −40° F, while the temperature over the sea is close to freezing (+32° F), so there is a temperature difference of 72° F or more between air over the water and over the ice, with low pressure along the edge of the ice. Warm air and ocean currents bring nearly twice as much warmth to the Arctic Ocean as is absorbed from solar radiation and the sea water never cools below about 29° F, so there is a constant source of warmth. Intense polar lows can develop to hurricane force in 24 hours or less. They then travel eastward in the northern hemisphere, but in two days or less they reach land and dissipate.

There is also a sharp contrast in temperature between tropical air moving toward the pole and polar air moving away from it. These airflows meet at the polar front, where air rises as part of the system of convection cells that forms the basis of the global circulation of the atmosphere (see box on page 4), and the rising air produces a belt of generally low air pressure. Winds are from the east on the poleward side of the polar front and from the west on the side nearest the equator. The temperature difference to either side of the polar front can cause fronts to develop (see box on page 56) with associated areas of low pressure (depressions). If the polar front is drawn as a line on a map, these fronts appear as waves along the main front, with the depressions at the wave crests. Such depressions form repeatedly along the polar front, often in "families", as frontal systems in which warmer, less dense air rises over cooler, denser air and the entire system travels eastward. When all the warm air has been raised clear of the surface, the front is said to be *occluded.* It is at this stage that an intense polar low may develop behind (to the west of) the occluded fronts if an extreme temperature difference triggers a local disturbance.

Where there is a large temperature difference in the air over the ice and sea close to the polar front, passing depressions intensify, the pressure within them falling. Air is drawn in from the adjacent region of higher pressure and the converging air rises. As it does so the Coriolis effect starts it rotating (see page 40). This increases the temperature differences at the surface, because the rotation carries cold air from the poleward side of the polar front into a warmer region and warm air from the opposite side into a cooler one. This is a *polar low.*

Compared with most depressions, a polar low is small. When it starts to form it may be no more than 600 miles across. Air flows into the low near the surface, rises, and flows away from the low at high altitude. This vertical movement intensifies the flow, as it does with a tropical cyclone, and intensification causes the low to shrink in size until, as a fully developed extratropical hurricane, it may be only 200 miles in diameter. At the center, atmospheric pressure may be less than 970 mb (the average sea-level pressure is 1,016 mb), a pressure comparable to that at the center of a fairly gentle hurricane, as hurricanes go. This pressure will generate sustained winds of about 45 MPH with gusts to 70 MPH, which is below hurricane force, but the pressure may be lower and wind speeds much higher.

Many high-latitude storms develop in this way, from polar lows, but they can also begin as revitalized tropical cyclones. When a tropical cyclone moves out of the tropics it crosses cooler water.

Water evaporates into it more slowly and this makes it weaken. Eventually it will die completely unless it encounters a cold front. When this happens, the warm air of the cyclone rides up the sloping boundary of the cooler air, and this forced lifting triggers a new bout of convection and convective warming as the rising air cools adiabatically and its water vapor condenses. The dying cyclone comes back to life and continues its journey, once more with the power of a hurricane.

No matter how it begins, an extratropical hurricane is much like a tropical one. It is circular in shape, with a clearly defined eye that is relatively free from cloud and in which the air is calm. This is surrounded by spiraling walls of cumulus cloud extending all the way to the tropopause. Above the hurricane, the outflow of air produces a thick tail of high-level cirrus clouds. Seen from space, it has the same "spiral galaxy" shape as a tropical cyclone.

There are differences, however. An extratropical hurricane has an even shorter life than a tropical one. It develops from a polar low to a full hurricane in 12 to 24 hours and, once formed, it moves at up to 35 MPH. This is about twice the speed of a tropical cyclone, and it moves in the opposite direction. Carried with the prevailing winds, tropical cyclones travel from east to west and high-latitude extratropical cyclones travel from west to east. In the northern hemisphere, their speed soon brings them to a large land mass where they weaken and die, so they last no more than 36 to 48 hours. There is much less land at these latitudes in the southern hemisphere, so storms there travel further and last longer. In the absence of land to reduce wind speeds and starve cyclones of the water they need to sustain them, winds between Antarctica and the southern continents are more severe than those at similar latitudes in the northern hemisphere.

When an extratropical hurricane does cross a coast, it brings heavy snow or sleet driven by ferocious winds. The winds are seldom strong enough to cause severe damage to buildings, but they can bring down power lines and uproot trees, and when they deliver drifting snow they can seriously disrupt transportation and communication systems.

Hurricane damage

By the time Cyclone Tracy moved away from Darwin, Australia, on Christmas Day, 1974, it had demolished about 8,000 homes. The city was almost completely destroyed.

After devastating the Bahamas, in late August 1992 Hurricane Andrew crossed southern Florida and Louisiana. With winds gusting to 164 MPH, it demolished some 63,000 homes in Florida. The towns of Florida City and Homestead were almost totally devastated. The hurricane also left 44,000 people homeless in Louisiana. Andrew was the costliest hurricane in American history. It caused damage in those two states estimated at around $25 billion.

A few days later, on the other side of the world, Tropical Storm Polly formed in the China Sea, then traveled westward to the coast of China. It killed 165 people and left five million without homes.

Wherever they occur, tropical storms and cyclones cause immense destruction when they cross land. Usually we think of the harm they do in terms of buildings demolished, but it is not only homes, offices, and factories that suffer. Hurricane Andrew destroyed at least half the Louisiana sugarcane crop, threatening farmers' livelihoods and reducing a great deal of their work to piles of useless, sodden vegetation.

Crop destruction is especially serious in the less industrialized countries, where the lost food may be difficult to replace and where a much larger proportion of the population work on farms than they do in North America, Europe, or Australia. Typhoon Cecil devastated crops in central Vietnam in May 1989. It also demolished around 36,000 homes, but houses can be rebuilt more easily than food can be obtained by a country that can ill afford to import it. In September of the same year, 1989, Hurricane Hugo swept over islands of the Caribbean and the eastern United States, destroying crops of corn and soybeans.

Like most tropical cyclones, Hugo also uprooted and killed trees. Orchards were ruined and forests laid waste. The Caribbean National Forest in Puerto Rico was badly damaged and the Francis Marion National Forest in South Carolina lost more than two-thirds of its trees and three-quarters of its endangered red cockade woodpeckers. In Charleston nearly all the trees were destroyed, and in North Carolina the city of Charlotte lost 20,000 of the trees that had once lined its streets and stood in its parks. The severe storm that crossed southern England in October 1987, with winds gusting to more than 80 MPH, uprooted and destroyed 19 million trees, including many rare specimens in the Royal Botanic Gardens at Kew, near London, which has one of the world's largest and most important plant collections.

The tree-lined streets gracing most of our cities and city parks, where we can relax, walk, or play, are important to us. If their trees are destroyed we feel the loss keenly. The trees will be replaced, of course, but it will be many years before the new saplings grow into the large, mature trees that soften the hard lines of streets and buildings and provide us with shade in summer. Not all hurricane damage can be repaired quickly.

The long-term effects on wildlife are usually less severe. Tropical cyclones and windstorms are natural events. They have occurred at intervals throughout history and the tropical forests have survived many. They blow down trees, but in natural forests this creates gaps that are soon filled. In tropical rain forest, trees blown down by the wind often sprout new growth, so a downed tree can recover by regrowing from itself, from its own ruins, as it were. There are few areas of rain forest, and perhaps none, that have stood for more than about 200 years without being disturbed by winds of hurricane force or by fire. Oddly, it seems that the tallest rainforest trees, with crowns that project above those of the trees around them, withstand hurricane-force winds better than the smaller trees.

Wind is moving air. It can damage trees and buildings because air is a physical substance that has weight and can exert pressure. It was Evangelista Torricelli who first confirmed that air can be weighed. In 1644 he invented the mercury barometer (see volume 6 for more details of his life). We use barometers to measure the pressure the atmosphere exerts, but it exerts that pressure because of its weight. In effect, a barometer is weighing the air above itself, in a column all the way to the top of the atmosphere.

Weight is the word we use for the force gravity exerts on a given mass. *Mass* is a property of all physical objects. They possess mass even if they are beyond the reach of gravity and weigh nothing.

If we say an object weighs one pound, for example, we mean by this that the mass of the Earth, which is very large, and the mass of the object, which is negligible by comparison, attract one another

Figure 24: *After Hurricane Andrew, several pine trees located in the Pinewoods development. Imagine the strength of the wind necessary to double over and snap trees in this manner.* (NOAA)

Kinetic energy and wind force

Kinetic energy (KE), the energy of motion, is equal to half the mass (m) of a moving body multiplied by the square of its velocity (*v*) (or speed). Expressed algebraically, $KE = \frac{1}{2}mv^2$.

This formula gives a result in joules if *m* is in kilograms and *v* is in meters per second. If you need to calculate the force in pounds exerted by a mass measured in pounds moving in miles per hour, the formula must be modified slightly to: $KE = mv^2 \div 2g$, where *v* is converted to feet per second (feet per second = MPH × 5,280 ÷ 3,600) and *g* is 32 (the acceleration due to gravity in feet per second).

with a force we measure as one pound. The weight of an object, then, is its mass multiplied by the gravitational force. For most practical purposes the Earth's gravitational attraction is the same everywhere, and it is usually the weight of an object which interests us. The obvious way to obtain the information we need is to give the gravitational force a value of 1. Then, when the two masses are multiplied together, the product is the mass of the object we are weighing (because $x \times 1 = x$). (In fact, the Earth's gravitational force varies from place to place, but the differences are extremely small and of importance only to scientists who measure them to learn more about the composition of the rocks beneath the ground surface.)

This useful trick, of declaring mass and weight to be equal, makes it easy to measure the mass of objects, but it works only so long as we remain on Earth. Move away from Earth, say to Mars, where the gravitational force at the surface is only 38% of that on Earth, and an object will weigh less. If it weighs one pound on Earth it will weigh a little more than six ounces on Mars. Its weight changes, but only because the mass of Mars is 38% of the mass of Earth ($x \times 0.38 = 0.38x$). The mass of the object remains the same no matter where it is. If you set off for Mars in your spaceship with a one-pound rock from Earth and threw it when you arrived, the rock would fly higher and further than it does on Earth but if it hit someone it would hurt just as badly as if you threw it in your own backyard.

When a mass moves it possesses energy of motion, called *kinetic* energy. If a moving object hits something, part or all of its kinetic energy is transferred to whatever it strikes. That is what can hurt and it is why air, which has mass like anything else, can cause damage if it moves fast enough.

Air can be compressed, so the mass of any given volume is very variable, but on average, at sea level, one cubic foot of air has a mass of about 1.2 ounces (which is 0.075 pounds). When it moves, as wind, its kinetic energy is equal to 0.075 multiplied by the square of its speed and divided by twice the acceleration due to gravity (see box). It is this energy that exerts a pressure force against anything in its path. You can feel it when you walk in a strong wind, and if the wind is powerful enough walking can be very difficult or even impossible.

Consider a gentle breeze blowing at 10 MPH. The force with which it presses against objects in its path amounts to about four ounces per square foot. This is sufficient to set a flag moving and leaves rustling, but you would barely feel it. See what happens, though, when the wind speed doubles. At 20 MPH the wind presses against objects with a force of one pound per square foot. Wind speed has doubled, but the force it exerts has increased fourfold. Now it can make small trees sway and you will certainly feel it. Increase the wind to 75 MPH, which is the minimum speed needed to qualify it as a hurricane, and it exerts a pressure of 14 pounds per square foot; a 100-MPH wind exerts a pressure of 25 pounds per square foot.

This may not sound like a very large pressure, but it is being felt on every square foot of an exposed surface. Suppose a mobile home is broadside to a hurricane wind. If the trailer is 30 feet long and 9 feet high, the side facing the wind has an area of 270 square feet. In a 75-MPH wind the force pressing against the whole side will be about 1.9 tons (3,780 pounds) and a 100-MPH hurricane will exert a force of 3.4 tons (6,750 pounds) against it.

Winds press hard against surfaces, but they also use leverage. Where there is a gap or a projecting surface the wind may press from a different angle, and this can tear structures apart. Roofs made from sheeting can be loosened along one edge then torn away as a single piece.

Ground-level winds do not blow at constant speed. The moving air is slowed by friction, due to its contact with the ground and structures on it, and deflected by hills, trees, and buildings. As it twists and turns, the resulting eddies create gusts. These are brief but often large increases in wind speed, and they have an important effect. If a steady wind pushes against a structure strongly enough to weaken it, a sudden gust may be enough to demolish it. A 75-MPH wind gusting to 90 MPH will press against our imagined mobile home with a force of 1.9 tons that now and then increases to about 2.8 tons and drops again. This will set the trailer rocking with increasing violence until it is overturned.

Much wind damage is caused indirectly. Once a large fragment has been torn free it may be thrown against another structure with enough force to damage it. This weakens the second structure, and perhaps fractures some of its surfaces, increasing the likelihood that the wind will complete its total destruction.

Trees are more often uprooted by gusts than by a steady wind. Rocking shakes their roots. Smaller roots snap, soil is loosened around the larger roots, and the trees are less firmly anchored in the

Figure 25: *A car overturned by Hurricane Andrew in Whispering Pines, a small community in Dade County, Florida.* (NOAA)

ground until a final gust is enough to tear the tree free and make it fall. Power lines, radio towers, and telephone poles are felled in the same way. In a forest, a falling tree may well bring down others, which strike still more.

Eddies due to friction are not the only cause of variations in wind direction and speed. The eyewall of a tropical cyclone consists of towering cumulonimbus clouds. These are the clouds that produce thunderstorms, and there is a great deal of thunder and lightning around the eye of the storm. Intense convection associated with the storms generates local disturbances where rising air rotates, as small cyclones surrounding the main one, and when they pass, the wind changes in both speed and direction, so structures are buffeted not only by strong gusts, but by gusts from different directions.

As though the gusting, hurricane-force winds were not hazard enough, tropical cyclones often trigger tornadoes around the eyewall. Like all tornadoes (see volume 2), these develop from the small cyclones in and beneath the storm clouds. Each tornado lasts for only a few minutes, and these are not ferocious compared with many tornadoes, but while they last the wind speed increases greatly and there may be many of them appearing and vanishing unpredictably.

When Admiral Beaufort devised his scale for wind force (see box on page 46) he related wind speed to its visible effects, originally on the state of the sea, but his scale ended with 75-MPH winds. He rated these as force 12 and called all winds greater than this

Saffir/Simpson Hurricane Scale

Number	Pressure in eye (mb)	Wind (MPH)	Storm surge (feet)	Damage
1	980	74–95	4–5	Trees and shrubs lose leaves and twigs; mobile homes damaged
2	965–979	96–110	6–8	Small trees blown down; exposed mobile homes severely damaged; chimneys and tiles blown from roofs
3	945–964	111–130	9–12	Leaves stripped from trees; large trees blown down; mobile homes demolished; small buildings damaged structurally
4	920–944	131–155	13–18	Extensive damage to windows, roofs, doors; mobile homes destroyed completely; flooding to 6 miles inland; severe damage to lower parts of buildings near exposed coasts
5	920 or less	155 or more	18 or more	Catastrophic; all buildings damaged severely; small buildings destroyed; major damage to lower parts of all buildings less than 15 ft above sea level to 0.3 mile inland

hurricanes. In his original, handwritten scale the admiral did not even attempt to describe a hurricane. He simply wrote "Hurricane!"

The scale was good enough for mariners who needed to know how much sail a ship should carry, because a wind of 75 MPH or more would quickly reduce any sail to tatters and probably carry away the spar to which it was attached and possibly the mast as well. No sail should be carried. The Beaufort scale is not much use to people on land who may find themselves in the path of an approaching hurricane and need to know whether it will destroy their homes. It is not even much value to modern sailors because they do not use sails. An additional scale is needed to start where the Beaufort scale ends. Several have been compiled, but the most widely used one is called the Saffir/Simpson Hurricane Scale (see box). When hurricane forecasters at the National Oceanic and Atmospheric Administration issue warnings it is the Saffir/Simpson scale they use to assign categories to hurricanes. Unlike the Beaufort scale, the Saffir/Simpson scale relates the damage a hurricane is likely to cause only partly to its wind speed. In addition to the ferocity of the wind, hurricanes also cause flooding and in most cases water does at least as much damage as the wind itself (see page 93). The scale also reports the atmospheric pressure in the eye, which is a useful indicator of the intensity of a tropical cyclone, because wind speed is directly related to the difference in pressure inside and outside the system.

We live on land and it is easy to forget what a tropical cyclone can do to ships. On September 11, 1989, Typhoon Sarah swept across the China Sea towards Taiwan. On its way it met a Panamanian freighter and broke it in two. In early November of the same year, 93 workers died in the Gulf of Thailand when Typhoon Gay capsized an American ship that was drilling for gas. An oil tanker was broken in two off the Philippines in October 1994 by Typhoon Teresa. Fishermen, working in much smaller boats, are especially vulnerable to tropical cyclones. Tropical storms killed 200 at Cox's Bazar, Bangladesh, in April 1994.

Far from land, a force 12 wind on the Beaufort scale makes the sea completely white and driving spray reduces visibility almost to zero. Beneath the spray, the waves themselves are huge. Their size depends on the wind speed, the distance over which the wind is blowing (called the *fetch*), and the length of time for which the wind blows. Waves are generated by the transfer of energy from wind to water and the energy the waves possess is

Figure 26: *A port bow view of the USS* Arleigh Burke *underway in rough Atlantic seas, March 31, 1993.* (Department of Defense)

proportional to their height, so the bigger the wave the more energy it has. As wind speed increases, more wind energy is transferred to the sea and the bigger the waves grow. A wind of 110 MPH can produce 30-foot waves.

It is only when the wind blows over a large fetch for many hours that the waves reach their maximum size, and the stronger the wind the greater the fetch and time that is needed for the waves to reach their maximum. This sounds contradictory, but energy can be transferred from air to water at only a certain rate. The greater the amount of energy to be transferred, the longer it will take.

In a tropical or extratropical cyclone, the winds approximately encircle the eye, so they blow from different directions at each point and are not constant enough to allow waves to develop fully. Waves travel in different directions and interfere with one another. It is the interference that makes the sea look as though it is boiling, but when several waves combine the result can be an extremely large wave. When two waves combine it may happen that the crests of one coincide with the troughs of the other. The two will then cancel one another and the water will be calm. Should the crests of both coincide, they will add to one another and the height of the combined wave will be roughly equal to the sum of the heights of the two individual waves.

It is difficult to predict the size and power of waves, but under any sea condition it is common for some waves to be much bigger than average. If 100 waves pass a particular point, for example, one of them can be expected to be nearly 6.5 times higher than the average and in every 1,000 waves there will be one that is nearly eight times higher.

There is a limit to the size of waves, however, because beyond a certain height a wave breaks as its own weight makes the upper part of the wave fall forward. The research ship *Resolution* reported 70-foot waves (measured from trough to crest) when it sailed through an extratropical hurricane in the Greenland Sea in 1994. Typhoon Cobra, which wreaked havoc with U.S. Navy Task Force 38 in December 1944 in the Philippine Sea, also produced waves 60–70 feet high. These are probably close to being the largest waves possible. Regardless, they are big enough. A 70-feet wave is about twice the height of a three-story house.

Waves travel, and those from a tropical cyclone can be felt at great distances. Larger than usual ocean waves in Alaska were once traced to storms near Australia, and waves formed near the Aleutian Islands are known to have reached California in about five days, having traveled at about 35 MPH.

Daniel Bernoulli and how hurricanes can lift roofs

Hurricane Marilyn raged through the U.S. Virgin Islands and Puerto Rico in September 1995. After it had passed, Wilfred Barry, a U.S. marshal who flew over the island of St. Thomas in a military jet to inspect the damage, was reported to have said there were no roofs at all left on the island. Every building had been stripped of its roof.

Hurricanes commonly tear roofs from buildings, especially roofs constructed from a few large sections with a shallow slope up to a ridge. Corrugated iron roofs are especially prone to flying away. So are the canopies over the fuel pumps at gas stations, located in exposed sites beside roads and held down only by ties to the tops of pillars. Slate or tile roofs are also destroyed, but piecemeal as the slates or tiles are loosened, then dislodged, one at a time.

You can imagine what happens. If the roof is made from sheeting, the wind pushes upward against a projecting edge, gusting repeatedly until it has detached that edge. Then it can bend the section sufficiently to provide a bigger surface on which to push. Slates and

Figure 27: During Hurricane Andrew, the County Walk development suffered numerous roof failures. (NOAA)

tiles overlap one another, so the roof surface is uneven. The wind works on this unevenness, penetrates the tiny air space between each slate or tile and the one overlapping it, and pushes up and back until the securing nails are withdrawn or broken.

Having devastated St. Thomas, the most seriously affected island in the group, Marilyn moved on to Puerto Rico. There it was Culebra Airport that felt the full force of the storm. One newspaper photograph showed a small airplane turned on its back, totally wrecked with its fuselage broken and its fin and rudder twisted to one side.

When you see pictures of hurricane damage it is not unusual to find some that depict light airplanes thrown upside down. These make dramatic photographs, of course, and one reason for the vulnerability of light airplanes is fairly obvious. Airfields are large areas of level, open ground where there is little or no shelter from the wind. If the airplanes are not moved into hangars or firmly anchored to the ground with cables, it is easy to imagine a strong gust catching the underside of a wing and flipping the plane onto its back.

In both cases, the picture is of the wind pushing upward, lifting the airplane or roof from below. No doubt this happens sometimes, but it is only one explanation and it may not account for the majority of such incidents. More commonly, the wind does not push wings and roofs from below, but first lifts them from above, and only then, when they are tilted so a large surface faces the wind, does the serious pushing begin.

The reason this happens was discovered in 1738 by the Swiss scientist Daniel Bernoulli (see volume 6 for details of his life). A physicist, mathematician, doctor, and botanist, Bernoulli was a truly remarkable member of an extremely remarkable family. His discovery, now known as the *Bernoulli principle* (or *law*), states that the pressure in a moving fluid (liquid or gas) is lower than it would be were the fluid at rest. His principle sounds wrong, because you would expect moving air to exert more pressure than still air, not less, yet its truth is very simply demonstrated (see volume 6 for no less than four demonstrations with which you can convince yourself). We exploit his principle in several everyday devices. A spray gun blows a stream of air across the end of a tube, the other end of which is immersed in a liquid. Reduced pressure in the moving air causes the ordinary (higher) air pressure to force liquid up the tube. A carburetor mixes droplets of fuel with flowing air in much the same way.

Indeed, you are probably familiar with the Bernoulli principle already. If you ride a bike, you know that when a car passes close while it is overtaking you the bike tends to be pulled toward the car, so you have to steer to avoid colliding or falling. It happens because the moving car drags air with it, so the air pressure between you and the passing car is lower than the air on the side of you away from the car, and this difference in pressure exerts a force pushing you and your bike in the direction of the car. Also, the faster the car is traveling the greater will be the force pushing you toward it. This is the Bernoulli principle at work, and the relationship between pressure and the speed of the moving fluid is what makes airplanes and roofs fly.

When a stream of air flows smoothly over a bulging surface, such as a ridged roof or the upper side of an airplane wing, it has further to travel than surrounding air that does not cross the surface. As figure 28 shows, however, it is not allowed any more time in which to do so. All the air must rejoin on the far side of the surface. This means the air flowing the greater distance must move faster and, therefore, the pressure it exerts will be smaller. Mathematically, Bernoulli showed that the pressure in a flowing fluid is proportional to the square of its velocity by the equation: $p + \frac{1}{2}rV^2 = $ a constant, where p is the pressure, r the density, and V the velocity of the air (or liquid).

While an airplane sits motionless on the ground, the air pressure is the same above and below its wings. Once it starts moving forward, air flowing over the shaped upper surface of its wings

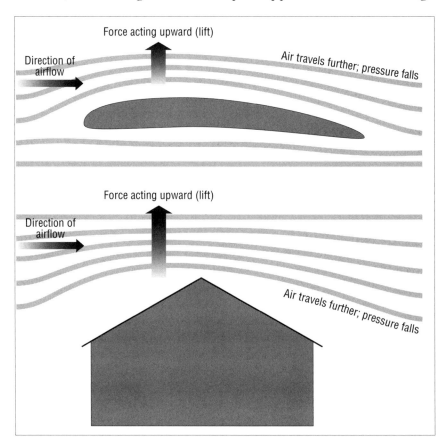

Figure 28: *The Bernoulli principle.*

travels further and its pressure falls. The faster the airplane moves the more the pressure above its wings falls until the difference in pressure above and beneath the wings exceeds the weight of the airplane. At that point it leaves the ground.

The airflow must be smooth (the technical term is *laminar*). If it is turbulent, countless small eddies form in which air flows in all directions. Pressure over the surface increases until it equals the surrounding pressure and there is no longer a lifting force. This is what happens when the airspeed of an airplane (its speed in relation to the airflow) falls so low that the plane stalls.

Suppose, though, that the airplane remains in one place on the ground, but is facing directly into the wind. Air is now flowing over its wings just as if the air were still and the plane were moving forward. Lift will exert a force on the wings. If the wind speed increases sufficiently, the lifting force may exceed the weight of the plane. It will not take off, of course, but it may rise from the ground, but unevenly. One wing may experience more lift than the other, the nose or tail may rise, and the plane immediately loses its lift and stalls. Completely unstable, the plane is at the mercy of the wind, which may well throw it onto its back. Once it is upside down it is much more stable, because any lift generated by the wind flowing over its wings will act downward, pressing it to the ground.

A building is not designed to fly, so it is less aerodynamically efficient than a plane, but the Bernoulli principle allows no exceptions. Wind, which is moving air, accelerates as it crosses the greater distance required by the shaped roof. Because it accelerates, its pressure falls by an amount proportional to the square of the wind speed. Inside the building, beneath the roof, the air pressure does not change, so the result is a difference in pressure that exerts a force acting upward on the roof. You might think of this as the wind pulling upwards, but it is more accurate to think of the roof being pushed upwards from inside the building, by the greater air pressure. It is not true, however, that this pressure difference can ever be so large as to make the building explode outward.

What the pressure difference can do is snap the ties holding the roof to the walls and lift the roof, or a section of it, clear of the building. Once free, the roof is even less stable than an uncontrolled airplane. It may be that one side will drop, tilting the roof in relation to the airflow. If the side facing into the wind drops, the lift over the section will increase and the roof will climb. If the opposite side drops, the full force of the wind will press against the exposed underside and the roof will fly horizontally. If the roof tilts to left or right in relation to the airflow, it may follow a curving path. In extreme cases the roof will tilt first one way, then another as it tumbles, twists, and turns unpredictably through a short, chaotic flight before crashing to the ground.

Figure 29: *Providence, Rhode Island, city hall engulfed by flood waters in a storm surge from the 1938 hurricane.*

Flipping airplanes usually harm no one, because no one is around, but flying roofs can do a great deal of damage. They may crash into other buildings, onto vehicles, or land on people.

Airborne slates and tiles are less dramatic, but even more dangerous. They can also generate enough lift to travel some distance and, because they are relatively small and there is so much else happening, people may not see them coming. A roof slate weighs several pounds and has sharp edges or, if it is broken, jagged points. Many people have been seriously injured, and some killed, by flying slates.

Storm surges

Hurricane Opal crossed Mexico and Florida in October 1995, causing damage that cost around $4 billion. It was not wind which produced the greatest devastation, however, but water. In this, Opal was a typical hurricane.

Tropical cyclones always bring torrential rain. This alone is enough to cause flooding, because the amount of rain falling in a very short period far exceeds the usual rate of precipitation. Natural drainage systems are able to remove rain falling only at the usual rate. Ordinarily, when rain reaches the ground, most of the water soaks down until it reaches an impermeable layer of rock or compacted clay. It collects above this layer as ground water, flowing slowly downhill and eventually enters streams and rivers that carry it away, eventually to a large lake or the sea. Together, the flow of ground water and surface streams and rivers link together to form a drainage network. If the rain falls very heavily, some of the water may flow across the surface because the impact of the raindrops batters soil particles, making a thin, compacted layer across the ground surface, so it is more difficult for water to drain downward.

This is what happens with normal rainfall, but when 20 inches of rain, or sometimes more, fall within a 48-hour period, the natural drainage network is overwhelmed. Tropical Storm Alberto delivered 24 inches of rain in some parts of Georgia in July 1994, and caused so much flooding in Georgia, Alabama, and Florida that all three states were declared national disaster areas. In October 1993, rain brought by Tropical Storm Flo caused mudflows that buried 200 homes in Luzon, Philippines.

When this amount of rain falls, water reaches the ground faster than it can soak downward. Most of it flows over the surface, moving rapidly downhill and accumulating on low-lying ground, but some finds it way into rivers. It makes their levels rise until the rivers overflow their banks.

Rain need not fall as intensively as this to cause floods, of course. Far less violent storms can cause flash floods and any prolonged period of heavy rain may deliver more water than natural drainage is able to remove.

If that were all a tropical cyclone could do it would be serious enough. People would expect hurricanes to cause at least some flooding. Unfortunately, it is by no means all they can do. They also cause the sea to rise 10 feet or more above its usual level, with huge waves that sweep inland, destroying everything in their paths. These sudden rises in sea level are called *storm surges*.

Opal hit the U.S. coast with 12-foot waves, and it was those and the flooding they produced which caused most of the damage to property. Storm surges can be larger and their consequences more serious. In September 1961, Typhoon Muroto II produced a 13-foot storm surge that sent sea waves rushing through the Japanese city of Osaka, and in late August 1992, Tropical Storm Polly caused a 20-foot surge at the Chinese port of Tianjin. Hurricane Frederic generated a 15-foot storm surge at the mouth of Mobile Bay, Alabama, in 1979.

Wind damage occurs because air has mass and when it moves it exerts pressure on objects in its path. This is familiar because all of us experience it. On a windy day you can feel the pressure of the wind. We do not usually feel the pressure of moving water, but it can be much greater than that of wind, because water is much denser than air. The mass of 1 cubic foot of air is about 1.2 ounces (0.075 pounds). The mass of 1 cubic foot of water is about 62 pounds. Moving at 20 MPH, 1 cubic foot of air exerts a pressure of about 1 pound per square foot, but 1 cubic foot of water exerts a pressure of 28 pounds per square foot. Gusts add greatly to the force of the wind, but the sea arrives as a series of waves that crash into structures, flow around and past them, and then return, flowing in the opposite direction, so they exert a push-pull force that is much more destructive than a steady push always in the same direction.

Three factors combine to produce a storm surge. The first is the fall in atmospheric pressure inside a tropical cyclone. This causes the sea level to rise beneath the eye of the storm. We are used to the idea that "water finds its own level." If one open-topped container full of water is connected by a pipe near the bottom to another that is half-full, water will flow from the full container to the half-full one until the level of water is the same in both. The two levels are the same because the air pressure is the same above the water in each container. The weight of the overlying atmosphere presses equally on each square inch of both water surfaces.

Over the ocean, the atmospheric pressure varies from place to place, so the weight of overlying air is not the same everywhere. Where pressure is high the sea surface is depressed, and where it is low the sea surface rises. "Sea level" is not the same everywhere. A drop in pressure of 1 millibar (mb) allows the sea to rise by almost half an inch. Beneath the eye of a category 1 tropical cyclone (see the Saffir/Simpson hurricane scale in box on page 85), the atmospheric pressure is 36 mb lower than the average of 1,016 mb, and in the deepest cyclone it may be 100 mb lower. These pressures raise the sea level by about 14 inches in a category 1 hurricane and by about 40 inches in a really intense tropical cyclone. As the eye approaches the coast, this is the amount by which the sea level will rise from this cause alone. This may seem a small rise, but if it coincides with a high tide it may be sufficient to flood low-lying coastal land.

Ocean tides are caused by the combined effects of the Earth's rotation and the gravitational attraction between the Earth, Moon, and Sun. As you know, if you fasten a weight to the end of a length of string and whirl it around in a circle, the weight pulls outward, making the string taut. This is due to what used to be called centrifugal force. In fact, it is the tendency of a moving body to continue moving in a straight line, counteracted by another force, in this case exerted by the string, which prevents it from doing so. On the Earth, gravitational attraction plays the part of the string and the oceans behave rather like the weight. They are pulled outward, as a bulge around the Earth.

Gravitational attraction from the Moon and Sun modify this effect. Because the gravitational force decreases in proportion to the square of the distance between bodies, the huge difference in distance from

Figure 30: *Submerged cars on downtown street in Providence, Rhode Island, flooded by 1938 hurricane.*

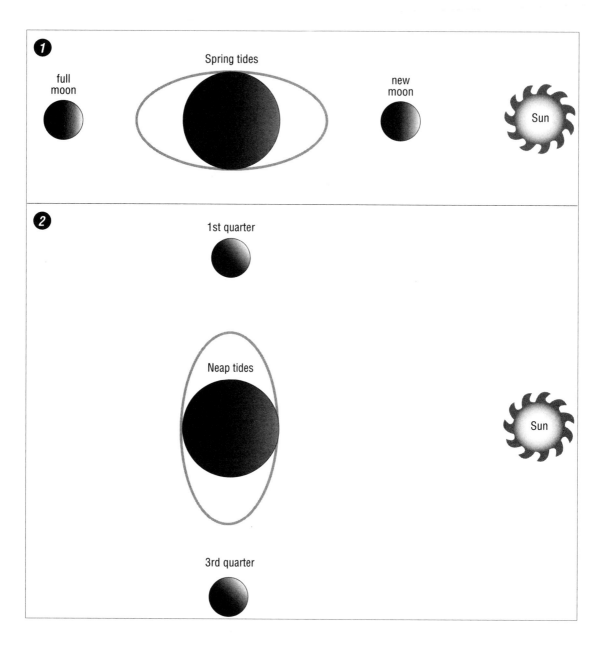

Figure 31: *Spring and neap tides.*

Earth to the Moon and the Sun mean the attraction between the Earth and Moon has about twice the force of that between the Earth and Sun. When the Earth, Moon, and Sun lie in a straight line, however, they add to the bulge due to the Earth's rotation. This produces spring (high) tides. When the Moon and Sun are at right angles to the plane of the Earth's rotation they produce neap (low) tides (see figure 31). Spring tides occur when the Moon is new and full, neap tides when it is at its first and last quarter.

Because the "bulge" is due to Earth-Moon attraction, it follows the Moon, circling the Earth every 12 hours and 25 minutes. The two crests are of equal size only when the Moon is directly above the equator.

The tides cause waves that travel across the oceans. They are only about 2 feet high, but when they approach a coast or an enclosed area of the sea, such as a bay, they are reflected. If the crests and troughs of the reflected waves coincide with those of the waves generated by the tides, there will be a very large tidal movement. In the Bay of Fundy, Canada, this resonance generates spring tides of about 50 feet. Because of its size and shape, the Bay of Fundy has the largest tides in the world, but they are considerable along most coasts bordering oceans. At Boston for example, the average tide is 9 feet, ranging from 12 feet at springs to 6 feet at neaps. Add, say, a 2-ft sea level rise due to low pressure to a 12-ft spring tide and the sea may flood low-lying coastal areas.

Tropical cyclones also produce huge, wind-driven waves, which are the second factor contributing to storm surges. The waves move across the ocean, outward from the center of the storm. To the right of the eye (in the northern hemisphere), the wind is strongest because it is blowing in the same direction as that in which the storm itself is moving; there the waves build into a "pile" of water markedly higher than the usual sea level. This "heaped up" water is likely to cross the coast close to, or just ahead of, the "bulge" beneath the eye.

The storm waves themselves, together with the dense cloud of spray whipped from their breaking tops, ride on top of the raised water. As the storm crosses the coast, onshore winds on the right side of the eye hurl this mass of water directly at the land, with immense power.

Low pressure that raises sea level and waves driven by the wind, both possibly adding to the sea-level rise due to high tides, clearly present a threat to coastal areas. Whether that threat translates into serious damage depends on the nature of the coast itself. This is the third factor contributing to storm surges.

Continents do not end abruptly where they meet the sea. Coasts are, in effect, hillsides. As you approach the sea you are moving downhill, and the shoreline marks the height the sea reaches on the hillside. The hill slope may be more or less steep, but it is always a slope, never a vertical drop. This is true even where there are high cliffs, with the sea crashing against their bases. The cliffs are made by the sea, as over thousands of years it has washed rocks away, cutting into the hillside, but at the foot of the cliffs the sea is usually quite shallow, and the submerged surface slopes seaward.

Sea waves are disturbances that move through the water. The water itself moves vertically (strictly, it moves in small circles) but not forward. Similarly, if you tie one end of a rope to a support and shake the other end, you can make waves travel along the rope, but the rope itself moves only up and down, not forward with the waves.

The distance between one wave crest and the next is the length of the wave, or its wavelength. Its amplitude is the height of each crest, and depth of each trough, above or below the level of the undisturbed water, and the height of the wave is the distance between a trough and a crest, which is equal to twice the amplitude. The steepness of a wave is its height divided by its wavelength. The time that elapses between two crests passing a fixed point is the wave period. Waves move in groups. At the front of the group, waves grow smaller and then disappear as their energy dissipates. More waves replace them, advancing from the rear of the group, then disappear in their turn. The group as a whole advances at half the speed of its individual waves, and the energy of the waves moves forward at the speed of the group.

As a group of waves nears a coast it enters increasingly shallow water. The speed and period of a wave are determined by its wavelength and the depth of water. When the depth of water is equal to half the wavelength, the vertical movement at the base of the wave is curtailed by contact with the seabed. This slows the forward speed of the wave, and as the water depth continues to decrease it slows it more.

The wave period (the time between the passage of individual wave crests) remains unchanged, however, because waves continue to arrive at the same rate from deeper water. If the forward speed of the waves decreases, but the same number pass a fixed point each minute, it follows that the distance between one wave and the next must have decreased. As the speed of the group decreases, so does the wavelength of its individual waves. The waves also continue to carry an undiminished amount of energy. As they slow, this is possible only if their height increases.

As waves approach the shore, they slow down but become higher, and the distance decreases between each wave and the next. There is a limit to the height a wave can attain. Although the water appears to move only vertically, in fact small "particles" of water are moving in circles. As the waves grow higher they also become steeper and the "particles" move faster. A point is reached at which the "particles" at a wave crest are moving faster than the wave itself. When this happens the wave becomes unstable, its crest spills forward, and it becomes a breaker.

Storm surges happen when these factors combine. Low pressure raises the sea level, carrying water to above the ordinary high-tide mark. Fierce winds produce large waves on top of the raised water. As these waves approach the coast, the sea becomes increasingly shallow, which makes the waves grow higher and steeper.

Every tropical cyclone is likely to cause a storm surge, but its size and seriousness in any particular place depends on the shape of the coast. If the shore shelves steeply into deep water, the waves are much closer inshore before they enter the shallow water that makes them grow bigger, so they never reach the size of waves approaching up a long, shallow slope. Many oceanic islands escape the worst effects of storm surges for this reason. They are the tops of submarine mountains or volcanoes that project above the sea surface, with sides that slope steeply. Along the east coast of the United States, on the other hand, the slope is shallow and large land areas are 10 feet or less above the mean tideline. Storm-surge waves can grow very large and travel quite a long way inland before they meet ground high enough to stop them. Bays and other partly enclosed areas can increase the effect still further by reflecting waves that can add to the size of incoming waves.

Storm surges also produce sea currents that flow with considerable force along coasts. These can cause severe coastal erosion. Sometimes they can wash away highways built close to the shore.

Torrential rain and storm surges make water by far the most dangerous aspect of a hurricane.

Historic hurricanes

Tropical cyclones are entirely natural events and nowadays we know quite a lot about them, although there is still much to learn. We have satellites to observe them from space, and when they strike land, television pictures of their effects are seen within a few hours in homes all over the world. People in distant lands give generously to help relieve the suffering they cause. We are keenly aware of the harm the weather can do.

This is a recent development, made possible by technological advances achieved in the last fifty years. It allows us to know more about these storms and to observe those that dissipate over the oceans without ever reaching land, but it does not mean tropical cyclones are more frequent than they have been in the past. People have been at their mercy throughout history, but the winds and storm surges, and the human tragedies associated with them, often affected remote communities. Unrecorded, the damage they did was repaired and in time they were forgotten, even in the places where they occurred.

Occasionally, though, a record has survived, sometimes because the storm marked the start of other events. In 1696, for example, a party of Quakers sailing from Jamaica to Philadelphia was caught in a hurricane and shipwrecked in the middle of the night on what is now Jupiter Island, to the north of Palm Beach, Florida. The event, and the hardships the travelers endured during the remainder of their journey, were described by one of them, Jonathan Dickinson, after whom a Florida state park is now named. We know of this hurricane only because it turned a fairly routine sea voyage into an epic overland journey.

Other storms are remembered because of the scale of the damage they caused. In 1099, for example, a hurricane moving through the English Channel produced a storm surge that killed 100,000 people along the English and Dutch coasts. At that time the population was less than 10% of its present size, so the loss of 100,000 people then would be equivalent to the loss of one million today. Quite apart from the innumerable personal tragedies such a disaster represents, it would have caused major economic disruption, producing a shortage of labor leading to wage rises over a large area. It is no wonder the catastrophe was remembered. Another storm entered history because of the awe-inspiring scale of its destruction. This happened on December 21, 1674, when the wind uprooted entire forests in Scotland. Only winds of hurricane force could cause such widespread devastation, but that is as much as we know.

We know much more about the hurricane which crossed southern England in 1703, because Daniel Defoe (1660–1731), the author of *Robinson Crusoe*, wrote a description of it. After an autumn of tremendous storms, hurricane winds began to blow on November 24 and reached their greatest intensity on November 26 and 27. According to Defoe, people were afraid to go outdoors or to go to bed. Perhaps they were wise to remain indoors and alert. The Bishop of Bath and Wells died in his bed when a chimney fell on him. Along the south coast, Eddystone Lighthouse, off Plymouth, was washed away and 12 warships were sunk. The rivers Severn and Thames flooded and as the storm moved east large areas were inundated along the coast of the Netherlands. In all, around 8,000 people lost their lives in the floods and 14,000 homes were destroyed. In Kent, in southeast England, 110 houses and barns were destroyed, and in one place 16,000 sheep were drowned. The damage in London alone was estimated to have cost £2 million (at 18th-century prices). This was thought to have been the most violent windstorm ever known in England, but another, on December 7 and 8, may have been stronger.

There were also hurricanes that affected the course of wars. In September 1854 the British army invaded the Crimea at the start of the 1854–56 Crimean War, and when the brief campaign the generals had planned failed, the troops were compelled to spend the winter there. The British fleet duly arrived with winter supplies, but the Russians had mined the harbor of Sevastopol and the ships had to anchor outside, in the Black Sea. On November 14 the supply ships were destroyed by a hurricane. This event caused severe deprivation among the soldiers.

That hurricane seems of minor importance when compared with the most famous hurricane in military history. The Crimean hurricane did not affect the outcome of the war, but this one, not a hurricane, but a typhoon from the China Sea, did, and for once its consequences were beneficial, at least for the Japanese. They called it a "divine wind," or *kamikaze*.

It happened in 1281. The Mongols, who at that time ruled China and Korea, had ordered the Japanese to submit to them. When the Japanese refused, a Mongol army set sail in Korean ships for the southernmost Japanese island of Kyushu. They overwhelmed Japanese defenders on the small islands of Tsushima and Iki and some Mongol forces managed to land at various places on Kyushu, but in numbers the Japanese warriors could contain. It was then that the typhoon destroyed most of the Mongol fleet, saving Japan from the main invasion force and probable defeat. People believed the *kamikaze* had been sent by the gods to save the Japanese from conquest by foreigners. The event became the subject of epic stories and led to a religious revival. This must be the only occasion of a typhoon inspiring religious celebrations.

Almost certainly, the *kamikaze* is the only tropical cyclone that has ever brought any benefit to anyone at all, and even then the price was a heavy one, paid by untold fatalities of Mongol soldiers and Korean sailors. Most such storms bring only death and destruction, sometimes on a vast scale. In 1876, the Bakarganj cyclone, moving north from the Bay of Bengal and across the islands in the Meghna (Ganges) Delta during the monsoon when the river was at its highest level, drowned 100,000 people in half an hour.

Measured in terms of the loss of human life, the worst tropical cyclone in the history of the United States lasted from August 27 to September 15, 1900. It formed in the Caribbean, crossed the Gulf of Mexico, and reached Galveston, Texas, on September 8. With winds of 77 MPH gusting to 120 MPH it does not sound the most ferocious of hurricanes, but like most hurricanes it brought a storm surge, and it was the water that caused much of the destruction.

Galveston is a port, and these days a vacation resort, on Galveston Island, a barrier island separating Galveston Bay from the Gulf of Mexico. Nowhere is it more than 3 miles wide, and its average height above sea level is about 4.5 feet. In 1900 the city had a population of nearly 40,000. It was a thriving and commercially important port handling more than two-thirds of the U.S. cotton crop and substantial amounts of grain.

The U.S. Weather Bureau had warned of an approaching storm, but the citizens of Galveston took little notice. By dawn on September 8 there was clear cause for anxiety. It was raining heavily, the wind was increasing, and the air pressure was falling rapidly. Some people left the island; others sought shelter in buildings in the city center. As the eye of the storm drew closer the sea level rose and by noon the bridges linking the island to the mainland were submerged, cutting off the only escape routes. During the afternoon huge, breaking waves destroyed buildings near the shore and the city was flooded to a depth of about 4 feet. Houses, most of them made from wood, were torn from their foundations by the wind. Many just disintegrated, sending planks and other debris flying through the air, some of it killing or injuring people who were trying to wade to safety. It was not until about 10 P.M. that the hurricane began moving away and the wind abated.

First thing the following morning people began to list the casualties and assess the damage. More than 2,600 homes had been destroyed and around 10,000 people were homeless. About 6,000 people had been killed and 5,000 injured. A few brick buildings remained standing, but the city of Galveston was largely reduced to piles of smashed wood and rubble.

Galveston declined in economic importance after that, although the destruction wrought by the hurricane was only one reason. As a port, Galveston was unable to compete with others on the mainland, especially Houston. A sea wall, 17 feet tall and 10 miles long, was built after the 1900 hurricane. A wide boulevard runs parallel to the wall, contributing to the relaxed appearance of a resort, but the wall exists for necessary protection. It helped protect the city when the next hurricane struck in August 1915. Despite the sea wall, the 12-foot storm surge flooded the city to a depth of 5 or 6 feet and 275 people died. The most powerful hurricane ever to batter Galveston occurred in September 1961 and once again the sea wall held. On that occasion fewer than 50 people died, although there was extensive wind damage and flooding.

Figure 32: *People looking through debris in Galveston, Texas in September 1900.* (Courtesy of Rosenberg Library, Galveston, Texas)

Water is always the principal enemy in a hurricane. It was water that killed most of the 1,836 people who died in America's second most serious hurricane of this century. It occurred in Florida in September 1928, when the winds drove the waters of Lake Okeechobee into populated areas. Levees were built to contain the lake after that disaster and the next time a hurricane crossed directly over Okeechobee, in August 1949, the water did not overflow and only two people died despite a strong hurricane, with winds of 110 MPH gusting to 153 MPH.

It was not as fierce as the "Labor Day Storm" of 1935, in which 408 people died in southern Florida. Winds of 150–200 MPH were estimated (no instrument could measure them) on some of the Florida Keys. The eye of that hurricane had an atmospheric pressure of 892.4 mb, the lowest ever recorded in the western hemisphere until Hurricane Gilbert in 1988.

Much of the land along the southeast coast of the United States is low-lying and flat. The shallow slope of the seabed causes storm-surge waves to grow large, and occasionally they are able to inundate low ground for a considerable distance inland. Despite warnings, many people died because they remained in their homes in low-lying areas of Louisiana during a hurricane in 1915, and in June 1957 a storm surge of more than 12 feet along

Figure 33: *Bodies of victims of the Galveston hurricane awaiting identification in a cotton warehouse set up as a temporary morgue, September 1990.* (Courtesy of Rosenberg Library, Galveston, Texas)

the Louisiana coast, produced by Hurricane Audrey, caused flooding as much as 25 miles inland.

An even bigger storm surge, of 24.2 feet, crossed the Mississippi coast at Pass Christian when Hurricane Camille arrived on August 17, 1969. That time the sea did not inundate inland areas, but in Virginia Camille delivered 27 inches of rain in 8 hours, driven by winds of 100 MPH gusting to as much as 175 MPH. The rain caused flash floods in which 109 people died and 41 remained unaccounted for. The final toll of casualties from both states was 255 dead and 68 missing. Flooding due to rain caused 30 deaths when a hurricane crossed Georgia, the Carolinas, and Tennessee in August 1940, while the wind caused 20 more.

States bordering the southeastern and Gulf coasts of the United States are most at risk from hurricanes, but more northern states are far from immune. In September 1938 a hurricane caused 600 deaths on Long Island, New York, and the southern part of New England. It traveled at 56 MPH, and winds of 121 MPH gusting to 183 MPH were recorded in Massachusetts. Other hurricanes caused damage in New England in 1944, 1954, 1955, 1960, 1972, 1976, and 1979. Indeed, in 1954 the region suffered three hurricanes. In August, Carol caused more damage to property than any storm recorded in the region to that time, much of it due to a storm surge that flooded many low-lying areas. Just as people were recovering from that disaster, Edna arrived in September, with a 120-MPH gust of wind recorded at Martha's Vineyard.

Hazel, in October of that year, was the third to arrive. It was one of the strongest storms ever to reach North America and also one of the biggest, affecting an area of 9,000 square miles. It destroyed three towns in Haiti on October 12, killing about 1,000 people, while at the same time drenching Puerto Rico, 500 miles away, with 12 inches of rain. It crossed the Bahamas, its winds strengthening to more than 120 MPH, and reached the U.S. mainland near Myrtle Beach, South Carolina, on October 15. The storm surge, of 17 feet in some places, caused devastation along 170 miles of coast. Then the hurricane turned north and, unusually for a storm once it was over land, it intensified. It produced a gust of 113 MPH in New York City, where it arrived during the heavily trafficked rush hour, and continued north into Canada.

Atlantic hurricanes are often severe, but they cannot match Asian typhoons for sheer ferocity. When Typhoon Vera crossed the Japanese island of Honshu in September 1959, it destroyed 40,000 homes, left 1.5 million people homeless, and nearly 4,500 dead. Japan, bordering the notorious China Sea, is especially vulnerable. About one-third of the city of Nagoya was destroyed by a typhoon that left one million people without homes in 1953, and the following year 1,600 people died when a typhoon struck Hokkaido. Fran, a typhoon that struck southern Japan in September 1976 with

100-MPH winds and 60 inches of rain, left 325,000 people without homes, and in central and northern Japan Typhoon Tad left 20,000 homeless on August 23, 1981.

All the countries bordering the China Sea are vulnerable and in most years up to 20 typhoons form there. Three million people lost their homes on July 23, 1980, when Typhoon Joe crossed northern Vietnam, for example, and flash floods and landslides caused by a typhoon in South Korea caused widespread damage in August 1982. South Korea endured two typhoons that month. The other, called Cecil, caused damage costing more than $30 million.

Not all Asian typhoons originate in the China Sea, of course. Many begin over the Pacific, then cross the China Sea as they move westward. In September 1984 Typhoon Ike killed more than 1,300 people and left more than one million homeless in the Philippines, then moved on to cause widespread damage on the Chinese coast in the province of Guangxi Zhuang, bordering the Gulf of Tongking. Storm surges along the Chinese coast are especially dangerous, because in many places, including the Gulf of Tongking, normal spring tides rise 20 feet.

The Philippines lie directly in the path of many typhoons, some of which generate very strong winds. Agnes, which killed 300 people and left 100,000 homeless in November 1984, brought winds of 185 MPH.

The extent of the damage caused by typhoons is not always due to flimsy construction. A typhoon is capable of demolishing sub-

Figure 34: *This photo depicts the raw power of hurricane-force winds. A piece of plywood was driven through the trunk of a royal palm near Homestead, Florida, during Hurricane Andrew.* (NOAA)

stantial buildings. Nagoya is a major industrial city, and Cyclone Tracy almost totally destroyed Darwin, Australia, on Christmas Day 1974. It was not a typhoon, but in November 1965 winds of 85 MPH demolished a cooling tower, 375 feet tall, at the Ferrybridge electricity generating station in England.

Cyclones from the Indian Ocean can also be extremely destructive. In June 1976 a cyclone destroyed almost all the buildings on the island of Masirah, Oman. On November 19 of the following year India suffered a much worse disaster when a cyclone struck Andhra Pradesh, in the east of the country bordering the Bay of Bengal. The cyclone produced a storm surge that completely washed away 21 villages and caused extensive damage in a further 44. That cyclone destroyed the homes of more than two million people and caused some 20,000 deaths. Another storm surge, of 10–15 feet, may have killed more than 10,000 people living on islands in the Meghna (Ganges) Delta of Bangladesh on May 25, 1985. About 45 villages were flooded, more than half a million buildings destroyed, and 1,500 people killed by a cyclone in Sri Lanka and southern India on November 23, 1978. In Madagascar, a cyclone with 150-MPH winds destroyed four-fifths of the town of Mahajanga on April 12, 1984 and in March 1994 a cyclone left 1.5 million people homeless in Nampula Province.

Tropical and extratropical cyclones form and intensify over the sea and at sea they are even more terrifying, and dangerous, than they are over land. Once over dry land they usually weaken, but over the sea they may still be growing. Given adequate warning, ships make for the relative safety of harbors, but that is not always possible. There may be insufficient time, and harbors may be full. Until recently, of course, the only warning mariners had came from their own observations and experience of what particular conditions of the sea and sky might herald. The *kamikaze* saved the Japanese, but only by destroying the fleet exposed to it in the China Sea. The English hurricane of 1703 sank 12 ships in the English Channel. Task Force 38 suffered severe losses when it sailed through Typhoon Cobra during the Second World War (see page 47) and the following summer, of 1945, 33 ships were damaged and 76 airplanes destroyed in another U.S. fleet under the same commander, Admiral Halsey, when it sailed through Typhoon Viper. In 1979 only 75 yachts completed the Fastnet Race between England and Ireland, out of 302 which started, because of a sea storm that intensified unexpectedly.

These were spectacular events, but others have entered history because they provide examples of heroism. Grace Darling (1815–1842) is perhaps the most famous. She was the daughter of the keeper of the Longstone lighthouse, off the coast of northeast England. When a storm drove the luxury liner *Forfarshire* onto rocks near the light on the morning of September 7, 1838, she saw there were survivors in a sea too dangerous for the lifeboat. Grace and her father rowed their own small boat a mile out to sea and rescued four men and a woman, and then Grace set out again with two of the men and rescued the remaining four survivors. Deservedly, Grace became a national heroine.

More recently, in December 1981, at the tiny village of Mousehole, Cornwall, in the far southwest of Britain, the entire crew of the Penlee lifeboat *Solomon Browne* was lost in a fierce storm while attempting to rescue the crew of a 1,400-ton coaster, the *Union Star*, which had been driven onto rocks. Each year since then the lights that decorate boats in Mousehole harbor and the buildings around it at Christmas are turned off for a time to commemorate the heroism of those lifeboat men, and their loss.

These were small incidents, though poignant. Others have involved tragedy on a larger scale. More than 500 casualties resulted when a number of ships were lost at sea during a hurricane in the Gulf of Mexico in September 1919. A cyclone in the Bay of Bengal capsized 200 or more Bangladeshi fishing boats on December 9, 1973. Most of the 1,000 people who died in that cyclone were drowned. More than 100 fishermen died when Typhoon Orchid struck South Korea in September 1980, and about the same number of fishermen died at sea during Hurricane Tico, in October 1983, off the coast of Mazatlán, Mexico.

Today, early warning allows people to be evacuated and skilled, well-equipped emergency services can reach disaster areas rapidly. Tropical cyclones cause fewer casualties than they did in the past, but their capacity to destroy property has not abated significantly. For the families and farmers affected, lost homes and possessions and crops are tragedies. Severe storms destroy lives, even of those they fail to kill.

How hurricane damage is predicted

Wind, rain, and the raging sea can wreak havoc, but their effects vary widely. A hurricane with 135-MPH winds that crossed Texas in 1949, for example, caused two deaths, but it remained in rural areas, destroying crops but not cities. Hurricane Beulah, in 1967, produced winds gusting to more than 100 MPH in Texas, but of the 15 deaths, 10 were due to floods and 5 to the 155 tornadoes the hurricane triggered. Hugo, on the other hand, in 1989, was the most destructive hurricane in U.S. history. With winds gusting to 220 MPH over the Caribbean islands and more than 80 MPH over the United States, accompanied by storm surges and tornadoes, Hugo killed a total of 43 people and caused damage costing $10.5 billion

Figure 35: *The ground station at Wallops, Virginia, that receives weather information from the GOES satellite and transmits it to the Miami Hurricane Center, which transmits relevant data to high-risk areas.* (NASA)

in the United States, as well as destroying almost all the homes on several of the islands it crossed.

These are among the most devastating hurricanes ever recorded. Others produce far less destruction despite generating winds, rain, and waves that may be just as fierce. Clearly, when local communities find themselves in the path of an approaching tropical cyclone they need to know the scale of the destruction they can expect. Emergency services, too, can function much more efficiently if they are given advance warning of the type and extent of the incident with which they will have to deal. This need was recognized long ago and the first U.S. hurricane warning was issued in 1873, when a tropical cyclone was seen approaching the coast between New Jersey and Connecticut.

Potentially dangerous storms can now be tracked for much longer and in more detail as they form, intensify, and move over the ocean (see page 32). At the same time their characteristics can be studied and their effects predicted. Much of the needed information is made available and adequate preparation can be made in time at least to minimize the number of casualties. The results have been dramatic. In 1925, hurricanes caused approximately 16 deaths for every million dollars of property damage. That number has been reduced drastically. For Camille, in 1969, there was one U.S. death for every $284 million of damage, and for both Gilbert in 1988 and Hugo in 1989, 1 death for every $2 billion of damage. (All damage costs are corrected for inflation and expressed in 1990 dollars.) Prediction allows time for life-saving preparation.

Although the ratio of deaths to property damage has improved and the actual number of deaths has decreased, the cost of hurricane damage to property in the United States has increased sharply during this century. An average of more than 800 people a year were killed by hurricanes between 1900 and 1910. By the 1990s the average was about 5. The cost of property damage, however, increased from almost nothing in the first years of the century to around $500 million a year in the 1930s and $2.6 billion in the 1990s. Improved precautionary measures account for the reduction in the number of deaths. The increasing risk to property is due to the rising popularity of Florida and the Gulf coast as places to live or vacation.

Measurements of the essential features of a tropical storm begin from the time it forms. At first they amount to an alert among meteorologists at the National Hurricane Center, in Miami, which is part of the National Oceanic and Atmospheric Administration (NOAA). When it appears that the storm is intensifying and heading

Figure 36: *The Geostationary Operational Environmental Satellite, also known as the GOES satellite.* (NOAA/ National Environmental Satellite, Data, and Information Service [NESDIS])

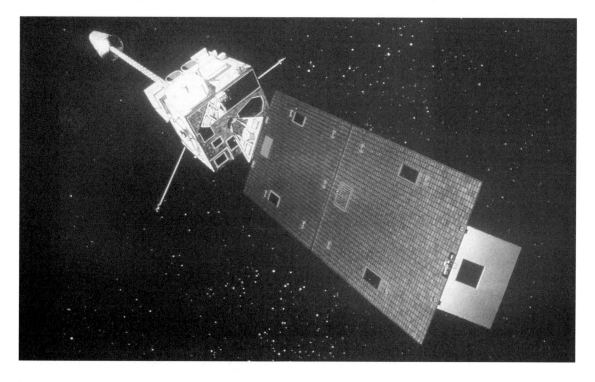

for land, closer observation begins and the resources devoted to its study increase greatly as it approaches.

The atmospheric pressure in the center is monitored because from this the meteorologists can calculate the wind speed. Cloud formations are observed because this allows the intensity of the rainfall to be estimated. The temperature is also watched closely because it is its warm rather than cool center that distinguishes a hurricane from a tropical storm. It is also important to measure the size of the entire storm system. This determines the width of the area it will affect as it moves inland and also allows scientists to calculate wind speeds at varying distances from the center.

As these measurements and calculations are being made, the track of the storm is being plotted. This plot, together with knowledge of the prevailing winds outside the disturbance and experience of the behavior of past hurricanes, provide a basis for the future track to be predicted. Hurricanes can change course for no apparent reason, so there is an inevitable element of uncertainty in the predicted track. To allow for this, warnings are issued for a belt considerably wider than the hurricane itself.

At this stage the meteorologists know the size and strength of the hurricane and have predicted where it will cross the coast, and from measurements of its speed, when it will arrive. Now other considerations become important. The pressure in the eye tells them by how much the sea will rise, and its time of arrival must be related to the state of the tide to anticipate the total rise in sea level. The size of sea waves can be calculated from knowledge of the wind speeds and must be related to the shape of the coast and slope of the sea bed. Together, the rise in sea level due to pressure, the tide, and the growth in the size of waves as they approach the shore make it possible to predict the size of any storm surges. The elevation of land behind the shore determines the distance the storm surges will penetrate inland, and when account is taken of the effect of the rainfall on natural drainage systems it becomes possible to predict the severity of any flooding.

Hurricanes are graded according to their eye pressure, wind speeds, and height of their storm surges, usually on the Saffir/Simpson scale of 1 to 5 (see box on page 85). It is now possible to assign the hurricane to a category and it is its category that determines the precautionary measures that should be taken before it arrives. The Saffir/Simpson category indicates the kind and extent of the damage the storm will cause, but only in general terms. Obviously, a hurricane that moves across a city center will cause far more damage than one passing only across sparsely populated countryside. No monetary values are attached to damage predictions, of course. Those come after the storm has passed and are based on valuations made by insurance companies. Warnings in advance of the storm are of such things as "mobile homes destroyed," "flooding to 6 miles

Figure 37: *Inside the National Hurricane Center in Miami.* (NOAA)

inland," or "extensive damage to roofs." They are meant to suggest degrees of severity without being specific.

Typically, the first "hurricane watch" warning, issued one or two days before the storm is forecast to arrive, affects a belt of coast and its hinterland about six times wider than the diameter of the hurricane. Much of this belt, to either side of the hurricane center, will miss the full force of the storm, although it may still experience strong gales. Because predictions of hurricane behavior are imprecise, it is quite likely that one side or other of the belt will escape entirely. This "overwarning" is not like "crying wolf" when there is no wolf. There is a hurricane, all right, even if happily it turns out to be somewhere else.

The actual diameter of the tropical cyclone determines the width of the belt that will be most seriously affected. With an allowance to either side for unpredicted deviations, a hurricane warning is issued for this belt. As the hurricane nears the coast this warning is regularly updated, with details of wind, rain, and storm surges as well as the speed and direction of its movement. The warnings must also distinguish the effects to either side of the center. Places near the eye wall and to the right of the track will experience the strongest winds (see page 3) and the heaviest rain will fall close to the eyewall.

If people act on the warnings, preparations for the storm will be completed by the time it arrives. Offshore installations, such as oil rigs, will have been evacuated. Fishing boats will be in harbors, tied up as securely as possible and their decks cleared of anything not fastened down. Larger ships will have moved into the most sheltered positions they can find. Factories in the path of the hurricane will have been closed and their machinery turned off. Offices will have been closed. All employees will have been advised to remain at home. Windows will have been boarded, on homes as well as shops and other business premises. People living on islands and along the coast will have been evacuated. Their numbers may have run into tens of thousands. If one or more cities are affected, the cost of these preparations runs into millions of dollars in materials, evacuation transport and accommodation, and lost production and if uncertainties in the strength or track of the hurricane mean the affected belt has to be widened the costs increase still more. Because of the high cost, warnings try not to exaggerate the risk.

Unfortunately, warnings are not always heeded. People are understandably reluctant to make expensive preparations and may hope they are lucky or, by the time they start to appreciate the danger they are in, they may have left it too late. Often, these are people with no previous experience of conditions in the eyewall of a major hurricane (one of Saffir/Simpson category 3 or higher) and it is easy to dismiss the warnings when the sky is blue, the air calm, and the hurricane, if it exists at all, is far away over the sea. Mostly, they are recent arrivals, enjoying the apparently reliable sunshine, warmth, and beaches around their new homes. They will have seen TV news stories about hurricanes, but these cannot describe what it is like to be there, what the hurricane really looks, feels, and sounds like, and the ease with which it can pluck homes from the ground and smash them to firewood.

Such people are unwise. It is not only their own lives they risk, but those of the emergency personnel who may have to rescue them. When a hurricane warning is issued it means a hurricane is approaching. Warnings are not issued lightly and must always be taken seriously and acted on appropriately.

How hurricanes are named and tracked

If a hurricane is heading your way you need to know how strong it is and when it will arrive. You do not need to know which hurricane it is, only that it is the one due to hit you tomorrow afternoon. Thinking back on the event in a few years' time, however, you might want to compare one hurricane with another. Then you would need a way to identify each of them. Of course, you could label them by their arrival dates. That is the only way we have of describing storms of long ago. The 1900 Galveston hurricane was just that, the 1900 Galveston hurricane.

Modern meteorologists need a better system because they often find themselves monitoring several hurricanes at the same time, all of them moving. At first they listed them by the latitude and longitude where they were first reported. Alternatively, they could have numbered them, perhaps with the year and the sequence for that year. Then you could have, for example, hurricanes 1:96, 2:96, and so on. Either system of numbering would work, but it was cumbersome. In the 1940s, when meteorologists began airborne studies of tropical cyclones, ships and aircraft communicated mainly in Morse code. This was satisfactory for letters of the alphabet, but it was not very good at dealing with numerals. With a dot (.) representing a short signal and a dash (-) representing a long one, —— —-... ——. ....., the Morse code for 1:96, is slow and can cause confusion.

Morse was abandoned when ship and aircraft radios started using voice communications. American meteorologists then listed tropical cyclones alphabetically, using the international phonetic alphabet for radios: Able, Baker, Charlie, Dog, etc. That was in 1951, but in 1953 a new international alphabet was introduced (Alpha, Bravo, Cocoa, Delta, etc.). This caused confusion, because one operator might report "Hurricane Dog," another "Hurricane Delta," and it would not be clear whether these were both the same hurricane or two separate ones. That system also had to be abandoned, and in 1953 meteorologists began using women's names instead.

The idea of giving hurricanes names was not new. In the West Indies people had long named hurricanes after the saint on whose day they struck and the practice had been adopted in other Caribbean islands. The storm that swept across Puerto Rico on July 26, 1825, for example, was known locally as Hurricane Santa Ana. Personal names were also being used elsewhere. "Saxby's Gale," which occurred in Canada in 1869, was named after a naval officer who was thought to have predicted it, and some meteorologists had been giving tropical cyclones women's names since the late 19th century.

Women's names remained in use until 1978, when some storm lists prepared for the eastern Pacific included men's names. In 1979 both women's and men's names were used to compile lists for the Atlantic and Gulf of Mexico and this still remains the practice, with male and female names alternating (Andrew, Bonnie, Charley, Danielle, for example). Also since 1979, the lists include names from non-English-speaking cultures.

The names are a substitute for the international phonetic code and so they are arranged alphabetically. In 1995, for example, the first Atlantic hurricane was called Allison, the next Barry, and so on down to Wendy. Tropical cyclones forming in the Atlantic and

Pacific are given names, but not those that develop in the Bay of Bengal.

Since different names must be allotted to Atlantic hurricanes and Pacific typhoons and all the names must follow an alphabetical sequence so each list does not contain two names beginning with the same letter, it will not take many years to use up all the names in the world. This difficulty is avoided quite simply. Lists are compiled in advance for six years and in the seventh year the first list is used again. The 1998 Atlantic hurricane list is the same as that for 1992, and the 1993 list will be used again in 1999. An exception is made, however, for hurricanes that were especially noteworthy. To avoid confusion, their names are retired and new names substituted the next time that list is used. In 1992, for example, the list began with Andrew. That name has been dropped and the 1998 list begins with Alex. Agnes (1972), Camille (1969), Gilbert (1988), and Hugo (1989) are among the names retired in recent years.

In 1998, hurricanes in the Atlantic, Gulf of Mexico, and Caribbean Sea will be called: Alex, Bonnie, Charley, Danielle, Earl, Frances, Georges, Hermine, Ivan, Jeanne, Karl, Lisa, Mitch, Nicole, Otto, Paula, Richard, Shary, Tomas, Virginie, and Walter.

Pacific lists are recycled in much the same way. Those for tropical cyclones in the eastern North Pacific (east of 140° W) are recycled on a six-year basis, like Atlantic names. Those for 1998 will be: Agatha, Blas, Celia, Darby, Estelle, Frank, Georgette, Howard, Isis, Javier, Kay, Lester, Madeline, Newton, Orlene, Paine, Roslyn, Seymour, Tina, Virgil, Winifred, Xavier, Yolanda, and Zeke.

There are four lists each for the central (from the international dateline to 140° W) and western (west of the dateline) North Pacific, but they are used differently. The first storm each year takes the name following the last one used the previous year. The last 1995 storm in the central North Pacific was called Nona and the first in 1996 was Oliwa, the next name in the list. When the last name in the fourth list has been used, the next will be the first in the first list. Confusion is avoided by attaching the year, so Oliwa was known as 1996 Oliwa.

Cyclones in the north Indian Ocean are not given names. Those in the southern Indian Ocean, South Pacific, and near Australia have names drawn from lists. In the southwestern Indian Ocean (west of 90° E) a fresh list is used for each year, the lists rotating in the same way as those used for Atlantic hurricanes. Elsewhere names follow on until each list has been used, in the same way as names used in the North Pacific.

A name is allocated as soon as the air around a disturbance starts rotating cyclonically (counterclockwise in the northern hemisphere) and its winds exceed 39 MPH. At this stage it has become a tropical storm and until it intensifies into a hurricane the name is prefixed with TS. Once it has grown into a hurricane the prefix is dropped and it is known simply by its name.

Until the late 1940s, spotting a tropical cyclone over the ocean was very much a matter of chance. A passing ship might report it, but unless it was close to a shipping lane it was unlikely to be noticed. In those days there were few airlines flying intercontinental routes and the aircraft they used lacked the range to fly far over the open sea. The most developed North Atlantic route, for example, went from New York or Montreal to London with refueling stops in Labrador or Newfoundland, Iceland or Ireland, and sometimes Prestwick, in Scotland. Aircraft were improving, however, and their numbers increasing. More advanced instruments allowed pilots to fly through cloud and meteorologists made use of them, often asking for reports on weather conditions, especially the height of cloud bases and tops. On military airbases, if it was uncertain whether conditions were suitable for flying, the day usually began with one pilot flying around the area of the field to check the weather. Pilots would not fly deliberately into a large cumulonimbus (storm) cloud, but even that was changing. Planes of the 1940s were stronger than those of the 1930s and had more powerful engines. Flying through a storm was not quite so dangerous as it had been.

By 1945, U.S. navy and army aircrews were flying meteorologists through tropical cyclones fairly routinely, gathering instrument readings from which the scientists came to understand the structure of these weather systems. Aircraft still fly scientific missions into hurricanes and typhoons.

These missions do not locate the storms, of course, but are directed toward storms that have already been identified. The early identification of atmospheric disturbances relies on satellites. The first weather satellite, TIROS (Television and Infrared Observation Satellite) was launched in April 1960 and within a few days had sent pictures of a typhoon no one had known existed, 800 miles from Brisbane, Australia. Today there are many weather satellites in orbit and new ones are launched at a rate of about two each year. The overlapping coverage of some forms a network, or "constellation," providing constant monitoring of the entire Earth.

Satellites can be placed in either of two types of orbit, called *polar* and *geostationary*. A polar orbit carries the satellite over both poles and in a series of orbits over the whole world. At a height of about 534 miles, the satellite makes a complete orbit of the Earth every 102 minutes. While it is doing so, the Earth is rotating beneath it. In 102 minutes the Earth turns 25.5° to the east, so with each orbit the satellite flies over a region 25.5° to the west of its previous pass. Satellites in geostationary orbit are directly above the equator, at a height of about 22,000 miles, and travel in the same direction as the Earth's rotation. Their orbital speed is the same as that of the surface beneath them, so they remain permanently over a particular point.

Figure 38: *The French Satellite d'Observation de la Terre, also known as the SPOT weather satellite, used for predicting hurricanes.* (CNES/SPOT Image)

Information from orbiting satellites passes to the organization that owns them, and all meteorological services are coordinated by the World Meteorological Organization, an agency of the United Nations. U.S. weather satellites are operated by the National Oceanic and Atmospheric Administration (NOAA) and observations of tropical disturbances are sent to the NOAA National Hurricane Center, in Miami.

Satellite photographs are studied closely. The meteorologists watch for the development of cumulus clouds with a wide layer of cirrostratus (thin, high-level, featureless sheets of cloud made from ice crystals). This combination indicates a strong convective system. Cloud movements are monitored to reveal the direction and strength of winds.

The scientists do not rely only on satellite images. Ships and aircraft also radio reports to them with information on atmospheric pressure and ways it may be changing, winds, and rain. If rain showers merge into steady rain, atmospheric pressure is falling, and winds are strengthening, the weather conditions will be classified as a tropical depression. As data continue to arrive at the Hurricane Center, any further intensification of the depression will be noticed almost as soon as it happens and the track of the system will be plotted carefully. If it becomes a tropical storm, with a cyclonic circulation and winds of more than 39 MPH, the next name in the list will be assigned to it.

When a tropical depression that has grown into a storm comes within a few hundred miles of the U.S. coast, aircraft join in the task of monitoring. The first to arrive are the "Hurricane Trackers" of the U.S. Air Force Reserve. Their job is to fly through the system measuring the distribution of pressure within it, wind speeds and directions, and locating the eye. Radioed back to Miami, this information allows interior details of the storm to be added to the charts. NOAA aircraft also join the team. Equipped with sophisticated instruments, these "flying laboratories" communicate with the NOAA Aircraft Operations Center in Miami.

Back at the Hurricane Center, the information from satellites, ships, and aircraft is fed into computer programs that predict the future behavior of the system. They estimate the likelihood that it will grow into a hurricane, and of what size and strength, and the track it will follow. If it is heading for an inhabited island or the U.S. coast, the relevant authorities are alerted.

Still closer to land, the tropical cyclone comes within range of onshore radar. There is a radar network covering the entire east coast of the United States, from Texas to Maine, and it extends seaward as far as the Lesser Antilles, the most easterly group of Caribbean islands, extending southwards in an arc with its northern end to the east of Puerto Rico.

Radar is electromagnetic radiation, the same type of radiation as visible light and radio waves, which is emitted from a transmitter and reflected from certain surfaces. The reflected radiation is detected by a receiver and provides two kinds of information. The first is an image, displayed on a screen, of the shape of the object scanned by the radar. The second is the distance to the scanned object. This is calculated by measuring the time that elapses between the emission of the signal and the arrival of its reflection. Like all electromagnetic radiation, radar travels at the speed of light, so the time it takes for the round trip reveals how far it has traveled.

Different radar wavelengths are used to scan different objects, and a wavelength of 10 cm (3.94 inches) is strongly reflected by water droplets. Once the storm is within range, radar can reveal its clouds and rain in great detail.

Nowadays it can do more, because the shore-based radars are being upgraded to Doppler systems. These measure the frequency of the reflected waves very precisely. The waves all travel at the same speed, but in 1842 the Austrian physicist Christian Johann Doppler (1803–53) made an interesting discovery, originally about sound waves but extended later to electromagnetic waves. If waves traveling at a constant speed are emitted by an object moving toward or away from an observer, their frequency will change. This happens because the distance the waves travel is changing. If the source is approaching, the frequency will increase, and if the source is receding, the frequency will decrease. With sound waves, increasing the frequency raises the pitch and decreasing the frequency lowers it. This is why the sound of a train rises in pitch as it approaches, then falls in pitch after it has passed. With light waves, increasing the frequency makes the light more blue, decreasing it makes the light more red. Astronomers have made use of this discovery for many years to tell how rapidly remote galaxies are receding from us (red-shifted).

Now meteorologists also use it with the help of systems that "translate" radar signals into colors on their computer screens. With Doppler radar they can add details of movement to the radar images they already have of the size of clouds and type and intensity of rain. They can tell how fast the storm is rotating because one side will be retreating and the other approaching. Color the retreating side red and the approaching side blue, based on the frequencies of the radar reflections from water droplets, and the rotation becomes clearly visible: the stronger the colors the faster the movement. The radar also reveals the direction in which the storm as a whole is moving and its speed.

Monitoring is now very advanced, but not all the tropics are covered so well as the seas off the eastern United States. Satellites observe the whole world, and ships and aircraft much of it, but planes equipped as meteorological laboratories, powerful computers, and radar networks are expensive. Until these are available in all countries that lie along tropical cyclone tracks, some communities will be less prepared than others for severe storms.

Will global climate change bring more hurricanes?

Throughout the late summer and fall of 1995 the hurricane trackers were kept very busy. It was the worst hurricane year for several decades. There was speculation that the increase in the number of hurricanes was linked to global warming, a worldwide increase in temperatures caused by increasing atmospheric concentrations of so-called "greenhouse gases," primarily carbon dioxide.

Such speculation was premature. There have always been more hurricanes in some years than in others. There were more than average in the five-year periods 1891–95, 1931–35, 1946–50, 1951–55, 1961–65, and 1966–70, but since then there have been fewer. Some scientists suspect the frequency of tropical cyclones rises and falls in a cycle of 30 to 40 years, in which case the large number in 1995 may mark nothing more than a return to a high-frequency stage of the ordinary cycle. Unfortunately, it was during the period of low hurricane frequency that so many people moved into coastal areas of the southeastern United States.

Just because a speculation is premature it does not follow that it is wrong, only that it is too soon to be sure. Most scientists believe that releasing certain gases into the atmosphere may affect the global climate, and some think they have detected the first signs of warming (though others disagree). Over the last 100 to 130 years the average temperature is believed to have increased by 0.54–1.08° F and the 1980s and 1990s have been the warmest periods on record. If the world does become a warmer place, there may be more tropical cyclones and their effects may be more severe.

So far, the changes are small. Average temperatures vary naturally from one year to another and even during the warm years of the 1980s and 1990s they remained within the limits of natural variability. The average temperature in 1995 was only 1.44° F warmer than the average for 1861–90 and 0.7° F warmer than the 1961–90 average. Such a small change is difficult to detect and even more difficult to interpret. It is suspicious that a sequence of warm years continued so long, and it is the kind of warming scientists expect if the global climate is changing as predicted, but the warming will need to go on for another 10 or 20 years before anyone can be certain it is due to the "greenhouse effect."

In a greenhouse, the glass allows solar radiation to enter, but prevents heat from escaping (mainly by trapping the warmed air inside), so air grows much warmer inside the greenhouse than it is

The solar spectrum

Light, radiant heat, gamma rays, X-rays, and radio waves are all forms of electromagnetic radiation. This radiation travels at the speed of light as waves. The various forms differ in their wavelengths, which is the distance between one wave crest and the next. The shorter the wavelength, the more energy the radiation has. A range of wavelengths is called a *spectrum*. The Sun emits electromagnetic radiation at all wavelengths, so its spectrum is wide.

Gamma rays are the most energetic form of radiation, with wavelengths of 10^{-10}–10^{-14} μm (a micron, μm, is one-millionth of a meter, or about 0.00004 inch; 10^{-10} is 0.00000000001). Next come X-rays, with wavelengths of 10^{-5}–10^{-3} μm. The Sun emits gamma and X-radiation, but all of it is absorbed high in the Earth's atmosphere and none reaches the surface. Ultraviolet (UV) radiation is at wavelengths of 0.004–4 μm; the shorter wavelengths, below 0.2μm, are absorbed in the atmosphere but longer wavelengths reach the surface.

Visible light has wavelengths of 0.4–0.7 μm, infrared radiation 0.8μm–1 mm, microwaves 1 mm–30 cm, then radio waves with wavelengths up to 100 km (62.5 miles).

outside. This is how the "greenhouse effect" acquired its nickname. The nickname is not really accurate, because although the result is similar, the reasons for it are quite different.

Most of the radiation we receive from the Sun is at short wavelengths, concentrated in the waveband we see as visible light (see above box). The atmosphere is almost completely transparent to this radiation, but some is reflected back into space from the tops of clouds and light-colored ground surfaces such as snow. Most of the radiation is absorbed, however, and warms the land and sea. The surface radiates some of its heat upward and air in contact with the surface is warmed and rises by convection. As it cools, the rising air also radiates heat back into space. Heat radiation, from the Earth and its atmosphere, is at long (infrared) wavelengths.

The atmosphere consists mainly of nitrogen (about 78%) and oxygen (about 21%). These gases are transparent to radiation at all wavelengths, but the air also contains very small amounts of other gases, which are not. Their molecules are larger than those of nitrogen and oxygen and, depending on their size, they absorb radiation at particular infrared wavelengths. Water vapor is the most important of these gases. Others include carbon dioxide, methane, CFCs (chlorofluorocarbon compounds, use of which is now being phased out because of their effect on the ozone layer), ozone, nitrous oxide, and carbon tetrachloride (a solvent formerly used in dry-cleaning, which is also being phased out). These are the "greenhouse gases."

The contribution each gas makes to the total absorption of infrared radiation is calculated as its *global warming potential* (GWP) and carbon dioxide is given a GWP value of 1. On this scale, methane has a GWP of 11, nitrous oxide 270, and CFCs and related compounds from 1,200 to 7,100.

Molecules of these gases absorb long-wave radiation, each at certain wavelengths. It warms them and they start radiating their own heat. They radiate in all directions. Some radiation goes upward, into space, but most does not. It goes sideways, eventually to be absorbed by other greenhouse-gas molecules and radiated in all directions again, or downwards. The overall effect is to warm the lower part of the atmosphere, which is where these gases occur. The gases are rather like a blanket and, like a real blanket, they allow some heat to escape through "windows," which are wavelengths at which no molecules absorb infrared radiation. A blanket on your bed keeps you warmer than you would be without it, but it does not keep your temperature rising indefinitely until your body cooks. In the same way, greenhouse gases keep the air warmer than it would be without them, but they do not make temperatures continue to rise until the oceans boil and the rocks melt.

People think of the "greenhouse effect" as a threat, but without it life on Earth would be very difficult and probably impossible. If the air contained no naturally occurring greenhouse gases, the average temperature at the surface would be about 5° F. Plants would not grow at this temperature and most of the oceans would be covered by ice.

The threat arises because we release greenhouse gases into the air, so the air contains more of them than it did naturally, and the concentration is increasing. If this continues, more long-wave radiation will be trapped in the atmosphere, causing the average temperature to rise. This is "global warming." However, the situation is far from simple. Carbon dioxide is the most important of the greenhouse gases we emit, not because it is more absorptive than the others, but because we release it in much larger amounts. It is produced whenever we burn anything containing carbon, because burning involves oxidizing the carbon to carbon dioxide ($C + O_2 \rightarrow CO_2$). All plant material, peat, coal, natural gas, and oil contain carbon. Of the carbon dioxide released by burning, however, only about half accumulates in the atmosphere. Scientists are uncertain about what happens to the remainder. Some dissolves in the oceans and some is taken up by plants in the process of photosynthesis, but a large amount cannot be accounted for.

Much still remains to be learned about the effect of warming on the oceans. They transport heat from low to high latitudes, so they have a very important effect on climates, but no one is really sure what will happen if the oceans grow warmer than they are now. Nor can scientists predict just how and where clouds will form. Some clouds reflect incoming solar radiation, others absorb outgoing infrared radiation, so it is very important to know how warming may affect cloud formation.

If temperatures rise, more water will evaporate from the surface, so cloudiness will increase and there will be more rain and snow, at least in some parts of the world. This might have several consequences. The polar ice caps might thicken, for example, because more snow would fall on them, so that rather than the ice caps melting and raising sea levels, sea levels might remain much as they are now, or even fall. More rain and snow falling in high latitudes, leading to an increased flow of fresh water into the sea from rivers and more falling on the sea itself, might reduce the density of the surface layer of the sea, because fresh water is less dense than salt. Were this to happen in the North Atlantic, it might interrupt the "Atlantic conveyor" (see page 8), in which case the warm North Atlantic Drift might cease to break away from the Gulf Stream. That would make the climate of northwest Europe much colder than it is now.

As it is, the warming observed so far is not spread evenly over the world. There is no clear evidence of warming in polar regions. Temperatures over the northwestern North Atlantic have risen less than those elsewhere, and have fallen in some places, and over the parts of the continents of the northern hemisphere the warming has been due to an increase in minimum nighttime temperatures, not in maximum daytime temperatures.

This is believed to be due to sulfur dioxide. In the air, sulfur dioxide (SO_2) attracts atmospheric water vapor and dissolves to form sulfurous acid (H_2SO_3) and then oxidizes to tiny droplets of sulfuric acid (H_2SO_4). These reflect incoming solar radiation and in moist air more water vapor condenses onto them, so they help form clouds. In both cases, by reflecting incoming radiation and increasing cloud formation, sulfur dioxide has a cooling effect. Volcanoes and several biological processes release sulfur dioxide, but it is also released when fuel containing sulfur such as certain qualities of coal and oil, is burned. There is much more industrial activity in the northern hemisphere than the southern, which may be why the northern hemisphere has warmed more slowly. It may also explain why nighttime minimum temperatures have risen in the northern hemisphere, but not daytime maximum temperatures. During the day, sulfuric acid droplets and cloud cool the surface by reflecting incoming radiation. Cloud also reflects outgoing heat radiated from the surface and at night, when there is no incoming radiation and the ground cools, this reduces the rate at which heat is lost. The combined effect is to make the days cooler and the nights warmer. Atmospheric sulfur dioxide has also been found to alter the track of the jet stream, leading to colder winds over the North Atlantic and North Pacific.

Most climatologists believe that by 2100 the average global temperature will have risen by 1.8–6.3° F. Sea levels have risen by 4–10 inches over the past century because water expands when it is warmed. Some scientists expect them to rise a further 6 inches by 2100, and others say they may rise an average of 13 inches with an outside chance they will rise 40 inches.

Studying the global climate is very difficult. Measurements of pressure, temperature, humidity, cloudiness, and so forth are now made in many parts of the world, but conditions in some large, sparsely populated areas are not reported so regularly. Reliable records of past weather conditions are even more scattered and none of them are continuous for very long. The longest is the "Central England" record, consisting of regular monthly reports since 1698, but it says nothing about the weather anywhere else. More records have been kept regularly since the last century, but most of them are local. It is hard to tell whether the climate is growing warmer or cooler without reliable records of past temperatures to make comparisons.

Predicting how warming on a global scale will affect particular areas is even more complicated. Scientists use the most powerful supercomputers in the world to calculate what is likely happen, but the results are meant to give only a general impression. They are not like the evening weather forecast.

It is important to remember the uncertainties, but few scientists doubt that the "greenhouse effect" is real and important and that global warming presents a threat to which we should respond by reducing the amounts of greenhouse gases we discharge into the air. If global warming does occur, an increase in the number of hurricanes may be one of its consequences, and the effects of the hurricanes may be more severe.

Although the sea is cooler in the North Atlantic and North Pacific, it is possible that average sea-surface temperatures have already risen in many parts of the tropics. Temperatures are predicted to rise more in high latitudes than in low ones, with little or no change at the equator itself, but there may well be some warming near the edges of the tropics, around latitudes 10–20° N and S, inside the belt where tropical cyclones form. Tropical cyclones can form only where the surface temperature of the sea is warmer than 80° F, and the frequency with which they occur today shows that this temperature is often reached. Only a small overall warming would be needed to increase, perhaps greatly, the number of days when sea-surface temperatures were suitable.

At the same time, temperatures over the continents would also increase. There warming might increase convection, leading to more thunderstorms. As these disturbances drift over the ocean they trigger the easterly waves (see page 33) that can develop into tropical storms and then cyclones. A quite small warming might be enough to increase the number of tropical cyclones forming each summer and fall. If so, the 1995 season may indeed become typical, although it is far too soon yet to tell whether it was due to global warming or merely part of a regular cycle.

Higher temperatures will make sea levels rise as the warmed water expands. Scientists do not expect the polar icecaps to melt within the next century. As always with hurricanes, water is as dangerous as the wind and even a small rise in sea level would make storm surges bigger.

It is possible, therefore, that global warming might make tropical cyclones more frequent and more destructive.

Protection and safety

If you live in an area that experiences tropical cyclones you should prepare for them well in advance. A little trouble taken in the winter and early spring could greatly improve your chances of escaping injury when the storm arrives. How do you know if your area is at risk? Ask people who have lived there for many years or check with the local newspaper or public library. If you live near a low-lying coast in a low latitude on the western side of the Atlantic or North Pacific or western side of the South Pacific, you can assume a hurricane or typhoon will visit you sooner or later. If you are new to the area, do not make the mistake of underestimating the power of a full-scale tropical cyclone.

Hurricanes, typhoons, and cyclones occur throughout the tropics. The precautions you can take apply anywhere. Wherever you live, the authorities will broadcast warnings and instructions before, during, and after the storm, but the warning system varies in detail from country to country.

Start by studying your local geography. Find out how high your home is above sea level, the height of the ground between you and the coast, and how storm surges have affected the district in the past. This will tell you what to expect from the sea. Torrential rains will probably makes rivers overflow. Where is your nearest river and is your home high above it?

You may have to leave home in a hurry, so work out the best route to high ground inland. Remember that if your only escape route crosses low-lying land or bridges, these may be impassable once the storm arrives, so you should plan to leave ahead of the bad weather. Try to arrange in advance to stay during an emergency with friends or relatives who live on high ground inland. The authorities will have allocated places in your area for use as emergency shelters. Find out where they are.

You will need to board up windows and secure external doors. Lay in adequate stocks of lumber, plywood sheeting, polyethylene sheeting, nails, and rope. Have high-quality flashlights and a reliable battery-powered radio, and make sure they are in working order and that you have spare batteries. Have a camping stove for cooking and plenty of fuel for it. A camping cooler box, with gel packs, will be useful for keeping fresh foods cool.

Prepare a first-aid box (any manual on first aid will tell you what it should contain). The box should be clearly marked and easily seen (ideally, paint it white with a large red cross).

You will need to store water. Keep enough clean, airtight containers to hold at least 14 gallons of water for each member of the household. Lay in supplies of dry or canned food. You will need enough to feed all of you for at least two weeks (including household pets). You will also need other household items, such as soap, toilet paper, toothpaste, and kitchen towels. If you are evacuated you will need blankets or sleeping bags.

Keep up with the house maintenance and gardening. Make sure there are no loose or missing roof tiles or slates. Keep gutters and drainpipes clear of obstructions. If there are any old or weak trees or shrubs near the house, remove them. Remove all weak branches from trees, trying to open up the trees so air can move freely through them.

When you learn that a storm is approaching, listen to broadcasts from your local radio or television station. Check the broadcasts frequently, if possible using house current to save the batteries. In the United States, the first alert will be a "tropical storm watch" or "hurricane watch" announcement. A storm means winds of up to 74 MPH, a hurricane means winds stronger than that. The warning will tell you when the storm or hurricane is expected to arrive. Usually it will give you about 36 hours to complete your preparations. You may also receive a "flash flood watch," warning of possible flooding.

See whether your car has a full fuel tank. If not, fill it. If you are taking medication, obtain an extra supply sufficient to last two weeks. Take out the materials you have stored for securing windows and doors and have them ready. If you have a mobile home, tie it down securely. Clear away any loose objects outdoors, such as garden furniture. Check your emergency supplies. Freeze the gel packs for your cooler box. Have a supply of cash.

A "tropical storm warning" or "hurricane warning" will be issued when the storm is expected within 24 hours or less. Board up windows. Leave the radio or television turned on so you will hear any instructions. Obey these at once.

If you receive a "flash flood warning" it means rapid flooding has either started or is imminent. You must move away from low-lying land immediately, and if your home is liable to be flooded, move upstairs. If possible try to travel in daylight, but in any case leave as soon as you can, because the roads may be crowded and some may be closed.

The warning may advise you to evacuate your home. If it does, do so immediately. You are likely to have to leave if you live within a few hundred yards of the coast, on an island, on the floodplain of a river, or if the land around your home has been flooded in the past by a storm surge. You should also leave if you live in a high rise because the hurricane may weaken the structure. Do not remain in a mobile home. No matter how securely you tied it down, the hurricane may be able to wreck it.

Before you leave, turn off the gas, electricity, and water supply. Unplug all electrical appliances.

Take personal identification with you, as well as important private documents and cash. If you are not moving to friends or relatives, try to book accommodation at a motel or hotel. Do not delay because many people will be seeking rooms in safe buildings. Let a friend or relative who lives far away from the affected area know where you are going.

Leave family pets behind. Make sure they are indoors and that you have left them ample supplies of food and water.

Do not go to an emergency shelter until you hear from the radio or television that the nearest one to you is open. If you do go to a shelter, take with you blankets or sleeping bags, toilet articles, your first aid box, a flashlight, and a radio. You will also need identification. Some cash may be useful, and you should take any important personal documents. You may be in the shelter for some time, so take things to pass the time, such as books, games, or cards. Do not expect the shelter to be comfortable or to find much privacy there. The authorities will do their best, but it is likely to be crowded and there may be no electricity.

Stay at home only if you have not been told to leave. If you are staying at home, unplug small electrical appliances and turn off the gas supply. Place fresh food in the refrigerator, turn it to full power, and open the door only when you must. Fill your containers with drinking water and fill the bathtub with water for washing. Close all doors and brace exterior doors so they cannot blow open. Keep listening to the radio and obey any instructions. You may be asked to turn off the electricity or water supply. Food in the refrigerator will remain safe to eat for a few days.

Move to the safest part of the building, taking your flashlight and radio with you. Keep as far as you can from windows. If possible, move into a room with no outside wall or, in a multistory building, close to (or beneath) the stairs. When the strong winds arrive, lie on the floor, if possible beneath some protection such as a strong table.

After a time, the wind may drop and the sky clear. Do not be tempted to go outdoors. This could be the eye of the storm. If so, the winds will return (from the opposite direction), possibly within a few minutes. Take no chances with the wind. Even if it seems safe, remember that hurricanes often trigger tornadoes and these could appear anywhere without warning.

When the storm has passed, a radio announcement will tell you it is safe to go outdoors. Until then, stay inside. If you are away from home do not try to return until you are told you may do so. You may have to produce identification before being allowed into your home. If your home has been damaged, do not enter until someone in authority tells you it is safe.

Outdoors, watch out for power lines that have been brought down in the wind. They may be alive. Be especially careful of pools of water with power cables lying in them. Look out for snakes: Floods may have driven them into the open. Keep clear of loose, overhanging objects and branches of trees.

When you are allowed back into your home, do not use open flames, such as candles. Use the telephone only if it is essential to do so. The emergency services need all the telephone lines. If you use fresh food bought before the storm started, be sure it is still edible. Dried or canned food is safer. Do not drink or cook food in tap water until you are told it is safe. When power is restored and the risk of fire has passed, you may be advised to boil water before use.

All tropical storms, hurricanes, typhoons, and cyclones are dangerous. Their destructive power is immense and their threat to life considerable, but with adequate preparation, a good warning system, and suitable precautions it is possible to survive them unharmed. Safety depends on knowing what to do, when to do it, and acting promptly.

INDEX

Italic numbers indicate illustrations.